RELIGIOUS STUDIES
(World Religions)

UNIT B579
JUDAISM 1

Contents

CORE BELIEFS

THE NATURE OF G-D	002
WHAT DO WE MEAN BY G-D?	006
MESSIAH & THE MESSIANIC AGE	011
THE MEANING & UNDERSTANDING OF 'COVENANT'	018
COVENANTS WITH ABRAHAM	025
COVENANTS WITH MOSES	030
THE LAW AND THE MITZVOT	034
BELIEFS ABOUT LIFE AFTER DEATH	042

SPECIAL DAYS AND PILGRIMAGE

SHABBAT	050
ROSH HASHANAH	058
YOM KIPPUR	067
PESACH	076
SHAVUOT	091
SUKKOT	096

MAJOR DIVISIONS AND INTERPRETATIONS

INTRODUCTION	107
ORTHODOX JUDAISM	108
CHAREIDIM	109
CHASSIDIM	110
MODERN ORTHODOX	114
RELIGIOUS ZIONISM	116
REFORM JUDAISM	121
LIBERAL JUDAISM	124
TWENTIETH CENTURY HOLOCAUST/SHOAH	128
THE LAND AND STATE OF ISRAEL	137

CORE BELIEFS

Religious Studies GCSE: Judaism 1

THE NATURE OF G-D

The nature of G-d is one subject about which there is very little dispute or disagreement. G-d's existence is accepted within Judaism without question. Maimonides does write, however, that every Jew has a personal responsibility to satisfy himself that he has no doubt that G-d exists. Knowing there is a G-d is thus considered the very first of the 613 commandments of the Torah. This can be fulfilled in many different ways

CORE BELIEFS

Religious Studies GCSE: Judaism 1

Some people look at nature and have no doubt that such a beautiful and complex universe could not possibly have created itself.

Some people look at history and conclude that there is just no way to explain how the Jewish people have continued to exist despite all the efforts to destroy them unless there is a G-d who is protecting them.

Some people look at philosophical proofs to satisfy themselves that there is clear evidence that G-d exists.

Some people don't need to look at all for it is so obvious to them that G-d exists that there are simply no questions to answer!

It does not really matter how you get there, but at the end of the day each Jew has a religious obligation to remove all doubt from his mind and to be absolutely certain that G-d exists. Maimonides goes on to say that this is the first commandment because, **if you are not sure that G-d exists, how can you keep any of the other commandments with any certainty that you are doing the right thing?**

Knowing there is a G-d also establishes that **there is a higher purpose** to life than just having as much fun as possible.

If G-d really does exist, then the only meaningful way to spend one's life is in the fulfillment of His commandments.

CORE BELIEFS

Religious Studies GCSE: Judaism 1

Once a person knows that there is a G-d, the next stage is to realise that there is only one G-d. Everything else is a creation and is under the control of G-d. This idea is captured in the first line of the Shema.

It is forbidden to worship idols, therefore, because idols don't have any power to help us. Whatever 'strength' a force may have comes from G-d anyway. The prohibition against worshipping idols is the second of the Ten Commandments.

The Talmud says concerning this that 'one who fears G-d need fear no man'. If G-d is in control of all, then nothing can possibly harm us without the 'permission' of G-d. A truly G-d-fearing person, therefore, will have no anxiety or worry in life at all. Such a person will trust in G-d for help and protection in every situation they find themselves.

Why did people worship idols?

In the ancient world, people recognised that there were powerful forces in nature without which life could not exist, e.g. the sun which provides heat and light, the moon which controls the tides, the rain which nourishes crops and the wind which transports seeds and dries the land. If these forces did not function properly, crops would fail and there would be famine in the land. In extreme cases, their malfunction could lead to floods or earthquakes. So the ancient civilisations worshipped these forces, made images to represent them and bowed down to them. They also built altars and offered up sacrifices to appease them.

CORE BELIEFS

Religious Studies GCSE: Judaism 1

Are there people who still worship idols today?

This all depends upon how you look at things. There is scientific evidence that all the planets exert an electro-magnetic force upon the earth, just like the moon exerts a force on the tides. Astrology is a belief that much of what happens on earth is controlled by the planets. This may or may not be true. But someone who believes the planets themselves are an independent force and not controlled by G-d would be considered to be an idol-worshipper.

Similarly, in the modern world, people also recognise the existence of powerful forces which dramatically affect most people's lives, e.g. there are economic forces which affect people's wealth, political forces which determine where power and influence lie, social forces which affect the way people live and military forces which, if not controlled, have the capability of destroying everything. The commandment not to worship idols includes the belief that none of these forces has an independent existence but that all are ultimately controlled by G-d.

CORE BELIEFS

Religious Studies GCSE: Judaism 1

What do we mean by G-d?

CORE BELIEFS

Religious Studies GCSE: Judaism 1

1. G-d is the creator of all.
Everything that exists in the universe only exists because G-d created it.

2. G-d has no physical form
Since G-d created the physical world, He is not part of it.

In the Talmud, a student asked his teacher: where is G-d in the universe?
The teacher answered: No! G-d is not in the universe. The universe is in G-d!
If G-d has no physical form, He is not bound by the physical world. We express this by saying that G-d is omnipresent.

This means that there is nowhere where G-d's presence cannot be felt, nowhere where a person may feel that G-d is not there with them. Whilst

it is definitely easier to feel G-d's presence in some places, such as in a synagogue or in Israel, the idea that G-d is omnipresent is a great source of security for it means that, no matter where we may be, G-d will always be with us.

Whenever the Tenach uses phrases like G-d's right hand or G-d's outstretched arm these are anthropomorphisms. This means that they are not to be taken literally. They are used to describe G-d's actions. What a human being needs a limb to do, G-d can do without a limb, e.g. the right hand is usually the stronger hand, so G-d's right hand is used to indicate G-d's strength. Similarly, when a human being stretches out his arm he is pointing in a certain direction. This is symbolic of giving direction and leadership so G-d's outstretched arm indicates His leadership.

CORE BELIEFS

Religious Studies GCSE: Judaism 1

3. G-d is neither male nor female

Male and female are physical characteristics, but G-d has no physical form so he cannot be specifically either male or female. The names of G-d most used in Tenach are Elokim, which is in a masculine form and the four-letter name (which Jews are forbidden to pronounce) which is in the feminine form. When describing G-d's strength, Elokim is used, but when describing his mercy and love then the four-letter name is used.

4. G-d is Omniscient

We said earlier that G-d was not bound by time. He therefore knows the past, present and future all at once, which is beyond human understanding. This teaches that G-d is all-knowing and all-wise. This is what omniscient means.

Knowing this helps us to be more honest. We may be capable of fooling people, but we cannot fool G-d! When we are honest with ourselves, this should motivate us to want to improve and become better people, so that we do not have to be 'ashamed' when being honest with G-d.

5. G-d is Eternal

This also something that is derived from the fact that G-d is not bound by time. He always was, He is and He always will be. Knowing this helps us to believe that we can rely on G-d. We can trust Him that He will always be there for us.

6. G-d is Omnipotent

If G-d is omnipresent and omniscient, it also follows that there cannot be anything within the creation that G-d cannot do. This means that G-d is also all-powerful. This is what omnipotent means. This is another aspect of us believing that we can rely on G-d because, if He is omnipotent, there is nothing too difficult for Him. No matter how dangerous or precarious a situation we may be in, G-d can always get us out of it.

CORE BELIEFS

Religious Studies GCSE: Judaism 1

7. G-d Is Merciful

Some people speak of Judaism as the religion of the strict law, which no human being is good enough to fulfill. This is a total distortion of Jewish belief. **Judaism has always taught that G-d's justice is tempered by His mercy,** the two qualities being perfectly balanced. Of the two Names of G-d most commonly used in the Tenach, one refers to His quality of justice and the other to His quality of mercy. The two names were used together in the creation story, teaching that the world was created with both justice and mercy

CORE BELIEFS

Religious Studies GCSE: Judaism 1

QUESTION

(a) What is a G-d? [1]

(b) Give two points that Jews believe about the nature of G-d. [2]

(c) Describe Jewish beliefs about how G-d operates. [3]

(d) Explain the importance for Jews of believing in G-d [6]

(e) "G-d is good." Discuss this statement [12]

CORE BELIEFS

Religious Studies GCSE: Judaism 1

MESSIAH & THE MESSIANIC AGE

CORE BELIEFS

Religious Studies GCSE: Judaism 1

What does the Torah say about the Messiah?

There is no direct reference to the Messiah in the Torah. When Jacob is lying on his deathbed, he refers to what will happen at 'the end of days' but nothing else is mentioned about that time. There is a Talmudic tradition that **Jacob was prevented by G-d from revealing this information** to his sons.

In Deuteronomy, however, there is an instruction that, at some unspecified future time, **Israel was to appoint a king.** The Hebrew word Messiah comes from the verb to anoint. Israel's kings were anointed. Orthodox Jewish teaching equates the Messianic figure with the king. **The coming of the Messiah, consequently, represents the restoration of the Jewish monarchy.**

CORE BELIEFS

Religious Studies GCSE: Judaism 1

There is a further reference to the 'end of days' at the end of Deuteronomy. This follows the blessings and the curses that will be sent to first reward then punish Israel for her conduct. When all these things have happened, the Torah continues, then G-d will ingather the exiles of Israel from the four corners of the earth. This ingathering represents the first task that the Messiah will accomplish.

What did the Prophets say about the Messiah?

The prophets speak mainly about how Israel will be exiled for her sins unless she repents and changes her ways. They also talk about the details of how, at the end of days, the Messiah will be sent to bring the Jewish people back to the land of Israel and to establish everlasting peace for all the world.

The main prophecies about the Messianic Age are found in Isaiah, Micah and Malachi. Jeremiah also talks about a 'new covenant' between G-d and Israel that will take place when the Messiah arrives and Daniel describes a series of dreams he had about when the Messiah would come.

CORE BELIEFS

Religious Studies GCSE: Judaism 1

What will the world be like after the Messiah comes?

Although there are different explanations about how the Messiah will come and what the world will be like afterwards, most Rabbis agree that **the Messiah will usher in an age of universal peace**. He will return the Jewish people to their land, rebuild the Temple and **all Jews will willingly follow the laws of the Torah**. The Messianic age will be followed by the **resurrection of the dead**. There will be reward for those who have lived a good life and kept the mitzvot and punishment for sinners. Judaism teaches that non-Jews who have kept the seven Noachide Laws are entitled to a reward just like Jews.

How will we know when the Messiah has arrived?

Throughout Jewish history many people have claimed to be the Messiah. Some of them attracted enormous followings. The Rabbis have always insisted, however, that until someone fulfils all these conditions, they cannot be identified as the Messiah and the Jewish people must continue to wait patiently for his coming.

There is a tradition that, **in every generation, there is one person who is worthy of being the Messiah**. If the generation is worthy to have the Messiah come at that time, his identity will be revealed. If the generation is not worthy, he will live and die as an ordinary person, after which somebody else will be the worthy one for the next generation.

CORE BELIEFS

Religious Studies GCSE: Judaism 1

How does belief in the Messiah influence Jewish life?

Some people reject belief in the Messiah claiming that it is simply a way of distracting Jews from their problems Instead of trying to solve their own problems, they wait for the Messiah to come and solve them for them.

On the other hand, these beliefs are a source of great comfort to those suffering poverty or persecution. They provide hope and trust that there will be a better future and the injustices that they suffer will one day be put right. For people on the brink of despair these are important ideas which fortify them with the strength to continue with the struggle for survival.

A belief in the Messiah also promotes a stable family life because it encourages parents to believe that their children will see a better world. It also offers an optimistic message that in the future the world's problems will be solved. Instead of encouraging a passive acceptance that the world cannot be improved, belief in the Messiah motivates one to action to improve the world now. Every little improvement brings the Messiah a bit closer!

Belief in the Messiah also promotes a more mature and responsible attitude to life amongst Jews, since you cannot just do whatever you like and forget about it. When the Messiah comes, everybody will have to give a full account of what they have done to hasten the Messiah's arrival.

CORE BELIEFS

Religious Studies GCSE: Judaism 1

When will the Messiah come?

Many people have claimed to be the Messiah. Some of them even had the initial approval of leading Rabbis and attracted enormous followings, but none have yet fulfilled all the required conditions. The Jewish people are still waiting for the coming of the Messiah.

False messiahs have done great damage for the Jewish people by raising expectations and then leaving their followers with a sense of deep betrayal. Today, some argue that the return of Jews from every part of the world to the land of Israel and the apparently miraculous establishment of the State of Israel mark the beginning of the Messianic era.

There is a Talmudic tradition that if every Jew observes one Shabbat, some say two Shabbatot, then the Messiah will come. This idea, together with the establishing of the state of Israel, has inspired many Jews to be involved in educational programmes geared to the non-religious to encourage them to return to the faith of their ancestors.

Generally, though, Judaism discourages spending too much time wondering when the Messiah will come. The main responsibility of a Jew is to make sure that their conduct in this world matches up to the highest standards set by the Torah. It is up to G-d to decide when to send the Messiah.

CORE BELIEFS

Religious Studies GCSE: Judaism 1

QUESTION

(a) Who is the Messiah [1]

(b) Give two points that Jews believe about the Messiah [2]

(c) Describe three things that will happen in the Messianic age [3]

(d) How does believing in the Messiah affect the life of a Jew [6]

(e) "Everyone should look forward to the coming of the Messiah" Discuss this statement [12]

CORE BELIEFS

Religious Studies GCSE: Judaism 1

THE MEANING & UNDERSTANDING OF 'COVENANT'

CORE BELIEFS

Religious Studies GCSE: Judaism 1

What is a covenant?

A covenant is an agreement entered into between two sides. The difference between a partnership and a covenant is that the two sides are not necessarily equal. Also, if one side breaks the covenant the other side remains bound by it. Biblical covenants usually involve G-d's protection and care in return for observing His commandments.

Covenants in the Tenach

Most of the covenants mentioned in the Tenach are between G-d and Israel. There are also covenants between people, for example David and Jonathan made a covenant in which Jonathan recognised David as the rightful successor to his father, King Saul and David agreed to protect Jonathan's family.

The first covenant specifically mentioned in the Tenach, however, is between G-d and Noah after the flood. G-d promises to protect and provide for all human beings and in return they would observe what have become known as the Seven Noahide laws.

CORE BELIEFS

Religious Studies GCSE: Judaism 1

Judaism teaches that not everyone has to be Jewish. Non-Jews are not expected to convert to Judaism or to keep the 613 commandments of the Torah. They are required to observe the Seven Noahide Laws that offer a basic code of morality. They are all moral and ethical rules with no ritual practices. They are:

CORE BELIEFS

Religious Studies GCSE: Judaism 1

1. Do not murder
Respect the integrity of each individual. This **establishes the basic human rights of all** to existence, regardless of race, colour or creed.

2. Do not commit adultery
Respect the integrity of the family unit. This establishes **a code of morality** and the necessity of marriage. There cannot be adultery if there are no marriage laws.

3. Do not steal
Respect the integrity of others' possessions. This establishes the need for **honesty in human relationships.** It also hints at the importance of personal responsibility for providing one's material needs. There can be no theft if there is no ownership.

4. Do not worship idols
Respect the integrity of G-d. This establishes the need for a knowledge and understanding of **G-d's complete mastery** of all the forces of the universe.

5. Do not blaspheme (take G-d's Name in vain
Respect the integrity of the relation with G-d. This establishes a concept of respecting those greater than ourselves and promotes **humility.**

6. Do not eat the limb of a live animal
Respect the integrity of the animal world. This establishes the principle that it is forbidden to cause any **unnecessary suffering to animals**. It effectively prohibits any wanton acts of cruelty, e.g. fox-hunting, bullfighting, random vivisection.

7. Establish courts of law
Respect the integrity of the community. This establishes the responsibility of each community to appoint three legal bodies: a **government** to determine the law; a **police force** to enforce the law; **courts** to punish those who break the law. In this way, each community will be able to maintain a system of justice which protects all those who abide by its laws.

By keeping these laws, Gentiles can ensure the basic morality and righteousness of this world and acquire for themselves a share in the world to come.

CORE BELIEFS

Religious Studies GCSE: Judaism 1

The two most famous covenants in the Tenach are between G-d and Abraham and between G-d and Israel.

In the covenant with Abraham, G-d promises to give his descendants the land of Cana'an as an eternal possession. Abraham commits to circumcise himself and all the males in his household and every boy that will be born in the future.

The covenant with Israel is made at Mount Sinai when G-d spoke and all the people heard. Israel commit to observe the laws of the Torah and G-d promised that they would be His Chosen People for all time.

There are other important covenants in the Tenach. One is between G-d and King David in which G-d promises that kingship will rightfully fall only to David's descendants. Another famous covenant is promised to the prophet Jeremiah. Jeremiah prophesised that the Temple would be destroyed by the Babylonians and the people would go into exile. But G-d also promised Jeremiah that one day He would bring His people back to the land and make a new covenant with them at that time.

CORE BELIEFS

How does the covenant concept affect the life of a Jew?

The concept of covenant gives a Jew the idea that he has a special relationship with G-d. This could be both good and bad.

It could be good because:
It encourages gratitude and humility by realising that G-d considers you important enough to have a special relationship with;

It encourages responsibility because, if G-d has picked you out for a covenant, you would want to do something for G-d in return;

It encourages the attitude of wanting to do for others just as G-d does for you;

It encourages loyalty to Judaism to keep your own side of the covenant.

It could be bad because:
It could make you arrogant if you think you are better than others with whom G-d has not made a covenant;

It could make you lazy if you think that G-d will give you preferential treatment;

It could make you selfish if you think other people are not really important at all;

It could make you concentrate on laws between man and G-d and neglect laws between man and man because you don't think they are as important to keep.

Religious Studies GCSE: Judaism 1

QUESTION

(a) What is a covenant? [1]

(b) Name two people that G-d made a covenant with. [2]

(c) What is particularly important about the covenant G-d made with Moses. [3]

(d) Explain the importance of the Noahide code [6]

(e) "The covenant concept is no longer relevant in the 21st century." Discuss this statement [12]

CORE BELIEFS

Religious Studies GCSE: Judaism 1

COVENANTS WITH ABRAHAM

CORE BELIEFS

25

Religious Studies GCSE: Judaism 1

Why did G-D make a covenant with Abraham?

There were ten generations between Noah and Abraham. By this time, almost everybody had forgotten the covenant that G-d had made with him following the flood. **Only Abraham was living the way G-d had wanted people to live.** G-d entered into a special relationship with Abraham, promising him that he would enter into a covenant with his descendants and that they would be His Chosen People for all generations.

There were two things that made Abraham special:

In a world in which almost everybody worshipped idols, **Abraham dedicated himself to trying to influence people to believe in G-d** and keep the seven Noahide laws.

Abraham's home was always open to receive guests. He was **exceptionally hospitable** to all

G-d made two covenants with Abraham, both of which are described in Genesis, the first book of the Torah.

Covenant Between the Parts

G-d promised Abraham that **his descendants would inherit the land of Canaan** (after which it would be known as the land of Israel). He then commanded Abraham to take a number of animals and slaughter them and then cut them in half. He also had to take two birds but they were not slaughtered. **Abraham was to walk between the parts of the cut animals.** A fire then came down from heaven and consumed the pieces, but the birds flew away. There are two levels on which this can be understood:

The animal pieces symbolise the **sacrifices** that Abraham's descendants would bring to the Temple to **atone for their sins.**

The animal pieces also symbolise the **wicked nations that would persecute and attempt to destroy his descendants**, who are symbolised by the birds. This was G-d's way of telling Abraham that **his descendants would always survive,** no matter how powerful their enemies might appear to be.

CORE BELIEFS

Religious Studies GCSE: Judaism 1

Abraham then fell into a deep sleep. G-d came to him in a dream and told him that his descendants would be exiled for four hundred years, **they would go down to Egypt but they would come out from there with great wealth.**

Covenant of Circumcision

When Abraham was 99 years old, **G-d commanded him to circumcise himself** and all the males in his household. Every boy that would be born from that time on was to be circumcised when he was eight days old (providing he was healthy enough). This teaches a number of lessons:

Circumcision is a reminder of the creation. When G-d created the world, He provided everything that human beings needed. They just had to complete the creation by looking after the world. Similarly, when a baby is born, he is virtually complete. There is just one small 'fixture' needed to make to complete him.

Circumcision is a reminder of the importance of morality. G-d could have arranged for a piece to be cut off any part of a baby. The place chosen is meant to symbolise the need for self-discipline and self-control in order to be a moral person.

Circumcision reminds parents of their responsibility to educate their children. Education is a very important part of Judaism. When a baby is born, parents are to take responsibility of their children's education straight away.

CORE BELIEFS

Religious Studies GCSE: Judaism 1

The covenants with Abraham emphasise a number of important principles of Judaism:

1. G-d chose the descendants of Abraham to be His Chosen People.
2. G-d promised them the land of Israel as an eternal possession..
3. G-d gives the opportunity to repent and be forgiven for one's sins.
4. Immorality is incompatible with Judaism.
5. Parents have a responsibility to educate their children.

CORE BELIEFS

Religious Studies GCSE: Judaism 1

QUESTION

(a) What is a covenant? [1]

(b) Name two covenants that G-d made with Abraham [2]

(c) What is particularly important about the first covenant G-d made with Abraham [3]

(d) Explain the main features of the second covenant G-d made with Abraham [6]

(e) "The covenants with Abraham are very important for Jews nowadays." Discuss this statment [12]

CORE BELIEFS

Religious Studies GCSE: Judaism 1

COVENANT WITH MOSES

CORE BELIEFS

Religious Studies GCSE: Judaism 1

Why did G-d make a covenant with Moses?

This was actually a covenant with the Israelites. Moses was the messenger through whom G-d made the covenant. This was the fulfilment of the promise G-d made when he made a covenant with Abraham.

Abraham had a son called Isaac. His birth marked the beginning of the covenant with Abraham being fulfilled. Isaac had a son called Jacob and he had twelve sons who were the originators of the twelve tribes. Jacob and all his family were forced to go down to Egypt because of a famine in Canaan and they settled there. After that generation had died, their children were made slaves by the Egyptians.

400 years after the birth of Isaac and 210 years after going down to Egypt, G-d sent Moses to lead the Israelites out of Egypt. Egypt was destroyed by 10 plagues and, after the Israelites left, the Egyptians pursued them to the Red Sea. G-d split the sea, the Israelites crossed and, when the Egyptians chased after them, G-d brought the sea back and the entire Egyptian army was drowned.

CORE BELIEFS

Religious Studies GCSE: Judaism 1

49 days after leaving Egypt, the Israelites encamped at the foot of Mount Sinai. G-d appeared to them on the mountain and spoke the first two of the 10 commandments. Moses then told them the rest of the commandments. The Israelites committed to G-d at that time and, after forty years in the wilderness, were given the Torah (the first five books of the Tenach) which contained the 613 commandments.

The Ten Commandments

This covenant, therefore, is about the Israelites' commitment to G-d and to the commandments of the Torah. At the time the covenant was made, they were told the Ten Commandments, which are the basis of all the other commandments. The Ten Commandments are:

1. I am the Lord your G-d [this means knowing that G-d exists]
2. Do not worship idols
3. Do not blaspheme/take G-d's name in vain
4. Remember the Sabbath day
5. Honour/Respect your father and mother
6. Do not murder
7. Do not commit adultery
8. Do not steal
9. Do not be a false witness
10. Do not be jealous

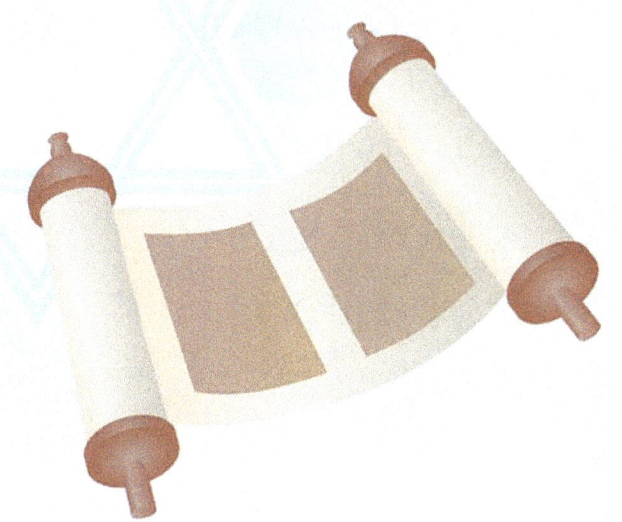

The commandments were deliberately written in two columns because, when Moses gave the people the Ten Commandments, they were written on two tablets of stone with five commandments on each tablet. The first five are commandments between Man and G-d and the second five are commandments between man and his neighbour.

CORE BELIEFS

Religious Studies GCSE: Judaism 1

QUESTION

(a) What is a covenant? [1]

(b) Name two of the Ten Commandments [2]

(c) What is particularly important about the first covenant G-d made with Moses [3]

(d) How does the covenant with Moses affect the life of Jews today? [6]

(e) "The laws between man and G-d are more important than those between man and man" Discuss this statment [12]

CORE BELIEFS

Religious Studies GCSE: Judaism 1

THE LAW AND THE MITZVOT

CORE BELIEFS

Religious Studies GCSE: Judaism 1

How does Jewish law work?

Judaism is not just a set of beliefs. It is a way of life, filled with laws and customs that affect every aspect of life. There are rules about what you do when you wake up in the morning, what you can and cannot eat, what you can and cannot wear, how to groom yourself, how to conduct business, who you can marry, how and when to celebrate festivals and Shabbat. Perhaps most importantly, there are rules about how to relate to G-d, to other people, and even to animals. This set of laws and customs is known as Halachah.

The word Halachah comes from the Hebrew word holeich which means to go or to walk. Judaism teaches that every Jew has a journey to take in this world and Halachah is the guide for how to make that journey. Some people might criticise this legalistic aspect of traditional Judaism, saying that it reduces the religion to a set of rituals lacking sincere involvement. If some Jews do observe Halachah in this way, then they are not observing the Halachah in the right spirit.

On the contrary, when properly observed, Halachah increases spiritual involvement because it turns the most trivial, mundane acts, such as eating and getting dressed, into acts of religious significance. Someone who observes Halachah carefully is constantly reminded of their relationship with G-d and of the importance of Judaism. It becomes an essential part of one's entire existence.

CORE BELIEFS

Religious Studies GCSE: Judaism 1

Isn't it sometimes inconvenient to follow Halachah?

Yes, of course. But if someone you love asks you to do something inconvenient or unpleasant, something you don't feel like doing, you would still do it. It is a very shallow and meaningless kind of love if you aren't willing to do something inconvenient for the one you love. How much more so should we be willing to perform some occasionally inconvenient tasks that were commanded us by G-d, especially when Judaism teaches that G-d never commands us to do anything that will not ultimately be for our own good.

Where does the Halachah come from?

There are three different sources for the Halachah:

From the Torah – laws given by G-d
From the Rabbis – laws introduced later to protect Torah laws
From customs – practices that have evolved over time

Halachah from any of these sources can be referred to as a mitzvah (commandment). The word mitzvah is also commonly used in a casual way to refer to any act of kindness. This usage of the word is not precise and can lead to misunderstandings. In serious discussions about Jewish Law, mitzvot are identified as being either mitzvot d'Oraita (an Aramaic word meaning from the Torah) or mitzvot d'Rabbanan (Aramaic for from the Rabbis) or minhag (a custom). Mitzvot from all three of these sources are binding, though there are differences in the way they are applied

Torah Laws

Some are clearly stated in the Torah but others can only be deduced by applying the rules for interpreting the Torah. It is an accepted tradition that there are 613 mitzvot in the Torah, but scholars disagree as to which are included. It is also an accepted tradition that the Torah contains 248 positive commandments, corresponding to the 248 organs/limbs of the body and 365 negative commandments, corresponding to the 365 openings of the body. In the Talmud, all these limbs and openings are identified.

CORE BELIEFS

Many of these 613 mitzvot cannot be observed nowadays. Many of the mitzvot concern sacrifices, which can only be offered in the Temple which does not exist today. Other mitzvoth concern the king and the Sanhedrin (the Supreme Court) which cannot be observed except in a religious Jewish State. Also, some mitzvot do not apply to all people or places. Most of the agricultural mitzvot only apply in the land of Israel and some mitzvot only apply to Kohanim or Levites. The Chafetz Chayim 1 observed that there are only 77 positive mitzvot and 194 negative mitzvot which can actually be observed outside of Israel today.

Rabbinic Laws

There are two different types of Rabbinic law:

Gezeirah: We commonly speak of a gezeirah as a "fence" around the Torah. For example, the Torah prohibits writing on Shabbat, but a gezeirah commands us not to even handle a pen or pencil, because someone who does so might forget that it was Shabbat and write with it.

Takanah: A takanah is a rule unrelated to a Torah law. It was instituted by the Rabbis for the public welfare. For example, the practice of public Torah readings every Monday and Thursday is a takanah instituted by Ezra. The mitzvah to light candles on Chanukah is also a takanah. The word is derived from the Hebrew root meaning to fix, to remedy or to repair. Its purpose, consequently, is to fix the spiritual standard of Jewish life. A famous takanah was instituted by Rabbeinu Gershom in the eleventh century. He forbade polygamy (marrying more than one wife). This takanah only applied to Ashkenazi Jews for Rabbeinu Gershom was the leader only of the Ashkenazi community.

---

1 Rabbi Yisrael Meir Kagan (1839-1933) the accepted spiritual leader of Orthodox Jewry in the last 30 years of his life.

Religious Studies GCSE: Judaism 1

Minhagim

A minhag is a custom that developed for some worthy religious reason and has continued long enough to become a binding religious practice. For example, the second, extra day of festivals was originally instituted as a gezeirah, so that people outside of Israel, not certain when the festival was due to start, would not accidentally violate the laws of that festival. After the mathematical calendar was instituted and there was no longer any doubt about the days, the added second day was not technically necessary. The Rabbis considered ending the practice at that time, but decided to continue it as a minhag. Today, the observance of two days Yom Tov carries the same strength as any Rabbinic law.

The word minhag is also used to refer to less stringent practices. For example, it may be the minhag in one synagogue to stand for a certain prayer, while in another synagogue it is the minhag to sit. Even in this looser sense, these customs do become binding on the individual. One must follow his own personal or community minhag as much as possible, even when visiting another community unless, of course, by doing so it would cause discomfort or embarrassment.

Are Rabbinic laws as important as Torah laws?

Jewish law includes both laws that come directly from the Torah (either expressed, implied or deduced) and laws that were instituted by the Rabbis. In a sense, however, even the Rabbinic laws can be considered derived from the Torah. This is because the Torah gives Rabbis the authority to teach and to make judgments about the law [1] so these Rabbinical laws should not be casually dismissed as merely the "laws of man" (as opposed to the laws of G-d). Rabbinical laws are considered to be as binding as Torah laws, but there are differences in the way we apply them.

1 See Deuteronomy 17:11 and Rashi's commentary

CORE BELIEFS

Religious Studies GCSE: Judaism 1

If two Torah laws come into conflict in a particular situation, we have to decide which law is followed. If a Torah law comes into conflict with a Rabbinic law, however, the Torah law always takes priority.

Example: Do we fast on Yom Kippur when it falls on Shabbat? These are both Torah laws, so rules of precedence must apply. Specific rules take precedence over general rules, so the specific rules of Yom Kippur fasting takes precedence over the general rule of Shabbat joy and so we fast on Yom Kippur when it falls on Shabbat.

Example: If one of the other fasts in the calendar falls on Shabbat, the rule is different. They are all Rabbinic observances and so the Torah law of Shabbat joy takes precedence and Rabbinic fasts that fall on Shabbat are moved to another day.

The other difference concerns the strictness of observance. If there is doubt concerning a Torah law, one must be strict. If there is doubt concerning a Rabbinic law, however, one can be lenient. .

Example: During the morning prayers, a man cannot remember if he said the Shema. Saying the Shema in the morning is a Torah law so he must be strict and say the Shema just in case he had not said it. If he cannot remember if he said a blessing before eating, on the other hand, since this is a Rabbinic law, he can be lenient. This is only if there is a doubt, however. If he knows he did not make the blessing, he must make it now.

CORE BELIEFS

Conclusion

In terms of importance, there is no difference between Torah laws and Rabbinic laws. All are equally binding, even minhagim that have become accepted. The difference only lies in a situation of doubt or where there is a clash. In those situations, Torah laws are clearly the more important.

CORE BELIEFS

Religious Studies GCSE: Judaism 1

QUESTION

(a) What is a Mitzvah? [1]

(b) Name two different types of Mitzvot. [2]

(c) Why is it important for Jews to observe the Mitzvot? [3]

(d) How does observing Mitzvot affect the life of Jews today? [6]

(e) "The Mitzvot from the Torah are more important than those from the Rabbis." Discuss this statment [12]

CORE BELIEFS

Religious Studies GCSE: Judaism 1

BELIEFS ABOUT LIFE AFTER DEATH

CORE BELIEFS

Religious Studies GCSE: Judaism 1

Judaism states very clearly that death is not the end of human existence. Judaism, however, is very much a religion that concentrates on life in this world rather than speculating on what happens after death, The general principle is that one's 'portion' in the next world is very much dependant upon one's conduct in this world. The principal 'belief' about life after death, consequently, is that one must concentrate on leading a good life in this world!

The Mishnah states that this world is like a lobby before the next world. Prepare yourself in the lobby so that you may enter the banquet hall.

Similarly, the Talmud says that this world is like the eve of Shabbat, and the next world is like Shabbat. He who prepares on the eve of Shabbat will have food to eat on Shabbat. We prepare ourselves for the next world through studying Torah and observing the mitzvoth.

The Talmud discusses life after death in many places. There is a reward for the righteous and a process of atonement for those who are not so righteous. This place of atonement is called Gehinnom. The maximum period of atonement is twelve months. Those whose failings cannot be atoned for in Gehinnom may be assigned for reincarnation in order to rectify that which was failing in one's earlier life. Finally, there is a specific 'sentence' for the totally wicked. They are called Gilgullim and their souls must wander this world until such time as their suffering is considered sufficient atonement.

Ultimately, in the Messianic age, there will be a Resurrection of the Dead in which all will return to life and live forever. Some say this only applies to the righteous.

CORE BELIEFS

Religious Studies GCSE: Judaism 1

What Happens After Somebody Dies?

According to Jewish tradition, there are a number of stages:

Between Death And Burial

When somebody dies, the soul leaves the body. **The Talmud states that the soul remains in the vicinity of the body until the funeral.** The soul is the real person, not the body. Death, therefore, is understood to be the time when we leave our bodies to go on to the next stage of our existence.

All the important functions of a person are in the soul, not the body. When we die, therefore, **we can see, hear, think and feel our emotions.** We can even speak (except that nobody can hear us!) but we cannot communicate with anybody. One thing that we do leave behind when we die is our yetzer hara, the evil inclination. Once we die, therefore, **we suddenly have complete clarity on what is good and what is evil** and we can immediately feel remorse for all the things we have done wrong. Also, seeing others do wrong would be disturbing and hurtful.

For this reason, there are many laws concerning how we are to respect the dead between death and burial:

After a person dies, **the eyes are closed, the body is laid on the floor** and covered, and **candles are lit** next to the body.

The body is never left alone until after burial as a sign of respect because the soul is hovering anxiously near it. Most communities have a body of volunteers called the **Chevra Kadisha** who take responsibility for this period. They assign people who sit with the dead body. They are called shomrim, which means guards. The **shomrim** may not eat, drink, or perform a commandment in the presence of the dead. To do so would be considered mocking the dead, because the dead can no longer do these things. **A man wearing tzitzit must tuck them in** for that too is mocking the dead to show them mitzvot that they can no longer perform.

CORE BELIEFS

Religious Studies GCSE: Judaism 1

One must be careful to only speak of respectful subjects in the presence of our dead body. Some have the custom to recite Psalms.

The body is purified through immersion in a mikveh so that it leaves this world in the same purity with which it entered.

Funeral

Judaism forbids embalming because it artificially preserves the body. It is **forbidden to look at the body** after death because that is not the person any more. It is just the 'garment' they wore in this world. It would be 'ignoring the soul' to do so.

Judaism also forbids cremation because this is artificially decomposing the body too quickly. The body must be laid to rest in the ground where it will decompose naturally. The Talmud states that **those who choose to be cremated do not return at the resurrection of the dead.**

In England, coffins are used for burial but they are not essential.
In Israel, bodies are buried just in shrouds.

At the time of the funeral, the soul leaves this world to go to judgement to establish its place in the next world.

Judgement

Judaism teaches that whilst the mourners sit shiva, **the soul is judged in the Heavenly Court.** All the good and bad deeds of its life are played before him and a decision is made by the court as to what place the soul will go now. There are a number of possibilities:

CORE BELIEFS

Religious Studies GCSE: Judaism 1

Gehinnom: Those judged to be basically righteous but in need of atonement for a number of outstanding sins will be sent to endure the purifying process of Gehinnom. The maximum amount of time any soul spends in Gehinnom is one year.

Heaven: Those judged to be righteous will enter Heaven immediately at an appropriate level, depending on how righteous they were. What exactly this is like is beyond our comprehension.

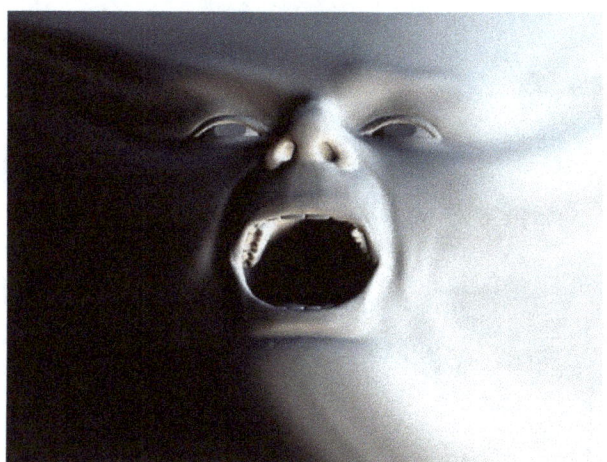

Reincarnation: Those judged to have wasted their lives may well be sent back to earth to live another life. It is interesting to note that being sent back to live again is considered a worse punishment than Gehinnom! This gives us some indication of how pleasurable Heaven must be.

Gilgul: Those judged to have been thoroughly wicked may be condemned to walk the earth as bodiless souls or to be sent back to earth as an animal, bird or even an insect as a means of atonement.

CORE BELIEFS

Resurrection of the Dead

Judaism teaches that the resurrection of the dead will occur during the Messianic Age. **When the Messiah comes to initiate the perfect world of peace and prosperity, the righteous dead will be brought back to life** and given the opportunity to experience the perfected world that their righteousness helped to create. Some say the wicked dead will not be resurrected. Others say they will be resurrected to suffer their final punishment at this time.

The Talmud states clearly that **the righteous of all nations inherit a portion in the world-to-come.** This means that Judaism does not restrict its heavenly rewards to those who are Jewish. On the contrary, Jews are judged by their observance of 613 mitzvot, but non-Jew are only judged on their loyalty to the seven Noahide laws.

Religious Studies GCSE: Judaism 1

QUESTION

(a) What is a Olam Haba [1]

(b) Name two ways in which Jews show respect for the dead. [2]

(c) Give three different things that Judaism believes may happen to someone after they die [3]

(d) How do beliefs about death affect the lives of Jews today? [6]

(e) "It is better to concentrate on this life than to be concerned with what happens after death." [12]
Discuss this statment

CORE BELIEFS

SPECIAL DAYS AND PILGRIMAGE

Religious Studies GCSE: Judaism 1

SHABBAT

For Jews, Saturday is no ordinary day. It isn't just the start of the weekend, it is the Shabbat; a day of complete spiritual serenity, dedicated to prayer, family and the Torah. The idea that people should take one day off their mundane activities comes from the beginning of the Torah, which describes how G-d created the world in six days and 'rsted' on the seventh day. The fourth of the Ten Commandments requires Shabbat to be honoured and safeguarded. Each week, in honour of G-d's creation and in line with the fourth commandment, Jewish people enjoy one day free from any work, secular concerns or creative activity.

SPECIAL DAYS & PILGRIMAGES

Religious Studies GCSE: Judaism 1

WHAT WORK IS FORBIDDEN ON SHABBAT?

The fourth commandment prohibits **melachah,** which is usually defined as creative activity. This is not the same as what we normally refer to as work. It is based upon the **thirty nine activities which were required to build the Mishkan** (the portable Temple built in the desert). These thirty nine activities (and anything that is similar to them) may not be done on Shabbat. Besides this, **the Rabbis later enacted many safeguards** to ensure that people do not accidentally break the Shabbat, e.g. one of the prohibitions is writing, so the Rabbis forbade picking up a pen in case you forget it is Shabbat and start writing with it. This Rabbinic law is called **muktzeh.**

In practical terms, the Shabbat laws mean that a Jew may not write, use money, electricity or their phone on Shabbat. One may not cook on Shabbat or travel by car, bus, train or plane. These laws might seem very restrictive, but in reality **they create an atmosphere of spiritual serenity**, undisturbed by the use of modern technology.

Shabbat begins at sundown on Friday afternoon, by which time the house has been cleaned and everybody is wearing Shabbat clothes. The mother/wife lights **two candles** which symbolise a peaceful home and then members of the family go to the synagogue. There is a special prayer called **Kabbalat Shabbat**, which welcomes the Shabbat and introduces the evening service. It consists of six joyous Psalms and a song called **Lechah Dodi** which was specially composed for this service the 16th century. The Psalm of the Shabbat then completes the Kabbalat Shabbat service.

SPECIAL DAYS & PILGRIMAGES

Religious Studies GCSE: Judaism 1

The family then gathers around the beautifully set table for the evening meal. The Talmud states that Shabbat angels accompany each family on Shabbat and a special song called **Sholom Aleichem** is sung before the meal to welcome them. **Eishes Chayil** is then sung, in honour of the wife/mother and in many families the parents give a blessing to their children. The meal begins with **Kiddush**, usually recited by the father/husband over a cup of wine.. This blessing describes Shabbat as a remembrance of the creation of the world and the exodus from Egypt.

After Kiddush, everybody washes their hands before the husband/father makes **HaMotzi** (the blessing over bread) over the **challos** (two whole plaited loaves) and gives everybody a piece to eat. The two challos recall the two portions of manna which the Israelites collected before Shabbat in the wilderness.

Now everybody enjoys a sumptuous meal during which they sing **Zemirot**, joyous Shabat songs and discuss ideas from the weekly Torah portion. At the end of the meal, the family and their guests chant Grace after Meals. In some communities there are acivities after the meal. A Friday night social gathering will be called an **Oneg Shabbat**, which means enjoying Shabbat.

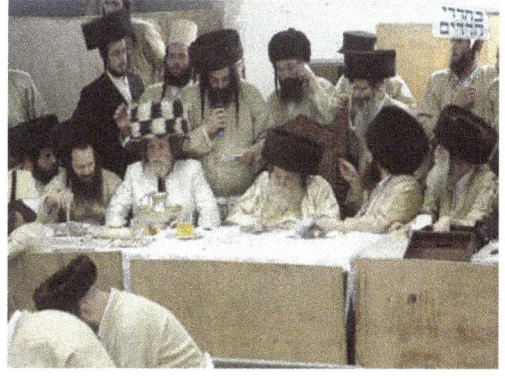

Chassidim often gather at the synagogue or home of their Rebbe for a **Tisch.** The word tisch means table and there is a large table at which the senior members of the community sit with the Rebbe. Everybody else stands around the table and sing in honour of the Shabbat. The Rebbe will eat a small amount of food and the contents of his plate are then shared by everybody.

SPECIAL DAYS & PILGRIMAGES

SHABBAT MORNING

In the morning, the synagogue service is much longer than on a weekday and some parts are sung together. The **weekly Torah portion is read** and this is followed by the **Haftorah**, a section from prophets which relates to that week's Torah portion. In many synagogues the Rabbi gives a **Drashah** (Sermon), also on the theme of that week's portion. At the end of the service, there is often a **Kiddush.**

The Rabbi makes the Shabbat morning Kiddush blessing for everybody and then cake and biscuits are eaten and sometimes there are drinks as well.

After the service, everybody goes home for the **second Shabbat meal**. Sometimes, Kiddush is made again (for those who weren't able to go to the synagogue) and the HaMotzi blessings on the two challot. The meal follows the same pattern as the previous evening meal with singing and discussion.

The afternoon may be spent resting, going for a walk or visiting family or friends. Some time may also be devoted to Torah study. Late in the afternoon, after the afternoon service comes the final, lighter Shabbat meal called **Shalosh Seudot** (or **Seudah Shlishit**) which means the third meal. This meal is quieter, the subdued atmosphere reflecting the sadness that the Sabbath is departing. It is traditional to sing in Hebrew the Psalm The Lord is my shepherd three times at the end of the meal. In some communities, this meal is held in the synagogue after the afternoon service.

SPECIAL DAYS & PILGRIMAGES

HAVDALAH

Sabbath ends when three medium sized stars appear in the sky. The evening service is followed by **Havdalah**, which means differentiation. Havdalah is a Kiddush that formally ends the Shabbat. It contains blessings over wine, sweet spices and a plaited candle. The spices symbolise our need to be refreshed in our sadness that Shabbat is over. The lit candle reminds us that work can again be done. The wine sanctifies the differentiation between Shabbat and the weekdays.

Religious Studies GCSE: Judaism 1

Possible Part D Question

How might observing Shabbat affect the life of a Jew?

A Jew wishing to keep Shabbat needs to make special arrangements with his employer to take time off work. In winter, one will leave early in order to be home and ready for Shabbat at sunset. One won't be able to work at all on Saturdays. This may put Jewish people at a disadvantage where employers are reluctant to grant them the flexible working hours that they require. Other employers, howver, may be impressed by the integrity of Jews who put their religion before their financial needs.

Jews have to live within walking distance of a synagogue so they can walk to Shabbat services. Jews therefore tend to settle in communities where they can all be within walking distance of the synagogue on Shabbat and festivals. This creates a warm community atmosphere. When travelling abroad, Jews must make sure that their schedule does not involve travel on Shabbat: that they can eat Shabbat meals somewhere and their hotel is near a synagogue.

Each Shabbat a Jewish family eats two large meals and one lighter meal. Often guests join the family. Since no shopping or cooking may be done from Friday afternoon until Saturday night, all the preparations for the festive meals must be made in advance. Boiling water is kept in an urn so that the family can have hot drinks throughout the day, lights are placed on a time switch so that they can enjoy electric light without using electricity and food is placed on a hot plate that keeps it warm. This means that each week time must be set aside for preparing everything for Shabbat

Shabbat has many positive effects on a Jewish family. A Shabbat-observant family spends at least one day a week together. No radio, t.v., phone or computer means that there are no external distractions and families spend time talking to one another sharing thoughts, ideas and problems.

The Sabbath is a time when a Jewish person is able to relax, to switch off the problems of every day life and regain a sense of self. It is a time to remember G-d and what He provides for us. It is also a time when family and community come closer. This may also help prevent assimilation since it keeps Jews together in a very close community.

Religious Studies GCSE: Judaism 1

Possible Part E Question

Is it necessary to observe Shabbat in the 21st century?

First write about 150 words explaining how Shabbat is observed, focusing on details you had no opportunity to explain in Parts A-D.

Some people might argue that whilst the Shabbat was once very important for Jewish life, it is now redundant. There were so few ways to relax before the growth of modern technology. But now we radio, television, computers, cinema and many different ways to listen to music, so there are plenty of other ways to relax. Also, they might feel that it is inconvenient and unpleasant to be told when and how to rest. They might argue that they have the right to choose to take advantage of modern technology to relax if they want to.

The observant Jew, on the other hand, keeps Shabbat because he/she believes that it is a Divine commandment. They enjoy the feeling that they are observing the same traditions that have been followed for thousands of years. Most Jews who keep Shabbat enjoy the serenity of the day and they look forward to the opportunity to spend time with their families unencumbered by the stresses of work. They argue that the meaning of a day of rest is not simply a day of doing nothing. It is a day of spiritual regeneration. It is a time for rebuilding bonds with the family and with G-d.

According to this point of view, abstaining from work is only the beginning. Modern technology merely provides distractions that get in the way of the real purpose of the day. Shabbat is a time for family, for prayer, for study, for thought and for reflection. All of that is best achieved without external aids.

SPECIAL DAYS & PILGRIMAGES

Religious Studies GCSE: Judaism 1

QUESTION

(a) What is the Sabbath? [1]

(b) When does the Sabbath take place? [2]

(c) Name three things which Jews cannot do on the Sabbath. [3]

(d) Explain why Jews celebrate the Sabbath. [6]

(e) "Regular weekly celebrations are more important for Jews than annual festivals." Discuss this statment [12]

SPECIAL DAYS & PILGRIMAGES

Religious Studies GCSE: Judaism 1

ROSH HASHANAH

SPECIAL DAYS & PILGRIMAGES

Religious Studies GCSE: Judaism 1

A MONTH OF PREPARATION

The month of Ellul is a time of self-examination in preparation for the High Holidays of Rosh Hashanah and Yom Kippur. This mood builds through the month of Ellul to the period of **Selichot**, to Rosh HaShanah and finally to Yom Kippur.

CUSTOMS ASSOCIATED WITH ELLUL

1. During the month of Ellul, **the shofar is blown every morning** at the end of the Shacharit (morning) service.

2. The shofar is **not blown on Shabbat**.

3. It is also **not blown on the last day** of Ellul, which is Erev Rosh haShanah, to make a distinction between blowing the shofar in Ellul, which is a Rabbinic law and blowing the shofar on Rosh HaShanah, which is a Torah law.

4. We blow the shofar in Ellul as a wake-up call, to arouse us from our complacency so we are ready for the period of repentance which begins on Rosh HaShanah.

5. On the first day of Ellul we begin to say Psalm 27. **LeDavid HaShem Ori** every morning and evening. Sephardim and Chassidim say it at the end of Minchah, Ashkenazim say it at the end of Maariv. We say this Psalm until Shemini Atzeret.

6. Ellul is also the time to begin **asking forgiveness for wrongs we have done to other people**. According to Jewish tradition, G-d cannot forgive us for sins we have committed against Him unless we have first asked forgiveness for sins we have committed against other people. Only the person we have wronged can forgive us for what we may have done against them. We have until Erev Yom Kippur to obtain forgiveness from others.

7. Many people **visit cemeteries** at this time to pray at the graves of the righteous or at the graves of members of their family. One reason for this is that it is the time of year when we are all concerned with thoughts of our own life and death.

8. Ellul is also the time when people **check mezuzzot and tefillin** to make sure the scrolls are still kosher for the new year.

SPECIAL DAYS & PILGRIMAGES

Religious Studies GCSE: Judaism 1

SELICHOT

Selichot are special prayers for forgiveness which are added to the daily cycle of religious services. Selichot are recited in the early morning every weekday, before shacharit. They add about 30 minutes to the regular Shacharit service.

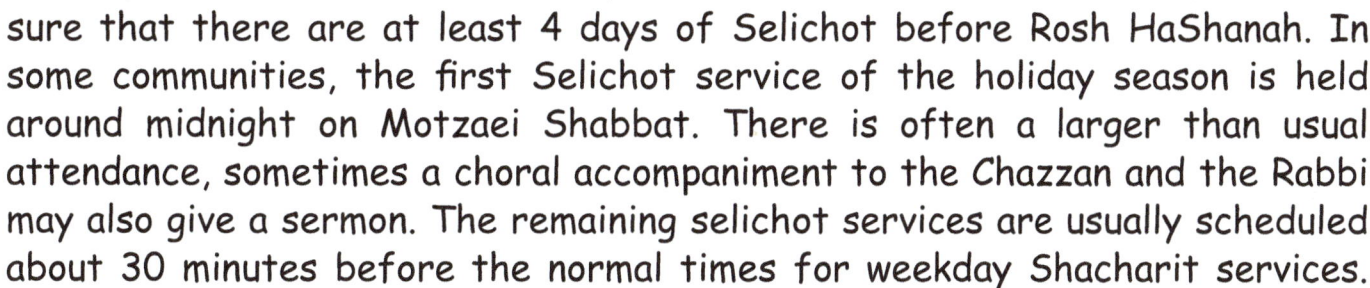

Selichot are recited every day (except Shabbat) from the Sunday before Rosh Hashanah until Yom Kippur. If Rosh Hashanah begins on a Monday or Tuesday, selichot begins on the Sunday of the week before Rosh Hashanah, to make sure that there are at least 4 days of Selichot before Rosh HaShanah. In some communities, the first Selichot service of the holiday season is held around midnight on Motzaei Shabbat. There is often a larger than usual attendance, sometimes a choral accompaniment to the Chazzan and the Rabbi may also give a sermon. The remaining selichot services are usually scheduled about 30 minutes before the normal times for weekday Shacharit services.

EREV1 ROSH HASHANAH

On Erev Rosh HaShanah the Selichot service is much longer, usually starting an hour earlier than the other Selichot services (which is an hour and a half earlier than normal Shacharit!) to emphasise the seriousness of Rosh HaShanah, the day on which everybody is to be judged for the coming year.

At the end of the service, there is a widespread custom to recite Hatoras Nedarim (the annulment of vows) in which we ask to be excused vows we may have inadvertently made in the past year and not kept. Those who were unable to say Hatoras Nedarim on Erev Rosh HaShanah may say it any weekday until Yom Kippur.

There is a widespread custom for men to immerse in a Mikveh as part of their preparation to enter the new year completely free of all impurity.

1 Erev means the day before

SPECIAL DAYS & PILGRIMAGES

Religious Studies GCSE: Judaism 1

QUESTION

(a) What is the month before Rosh HaShanah? [1]

(b) Give two practices that Jews perform during this month. [2]

(c) Describe three Jewish practices associated with the day before Rosh HaShanah. [3]

(d) Explain the importance for Jews of preparing for Rosh HaShanah [6]

(e) "It is not necessary to prepare for Rosh HaShanah." Discuss this statement. [12]

SPECIAL DAYS & PILGRIMAGES

Religious Studies GCSE: Judaism 1

ROSH HASHANAH

After Ellul is the month of Tishrei. The first two days of the month are Rosh HaShanah, the Jewish new year. This is both a festive and a solemn festival.

According to Jewish tradition, this is the day on which G-d created man. Rosh Hashanah, therefore, in a way is the birthday of the human race. On Rosh Hashanah, therefore, we are all judged for what will happen to us in the coming year. This is what we were preparing for during the month of Ellul. That is why it is considered appropriate to spend time in Ellul reviewing one's conduct of the previous year to see where improvements can be made. That way, when Rosh Hashanah arrives, we will know what to pray for.

The name Rosh Hashanah is not used in the Torah at all when referring to this holiday. The Torah refers to the holiday as Yom Hazikaron, which means the day of remembrance or Yom Teruah, which means the day of the sounding of the shofar.

YOM HAZIKARON

It is called this because G-d recalls all of our deeds on this day. It is also the day when we are supposed to recall all the areas where we are capable of self-improvement.

YOM TERUAH

It is called this because the shofar is blown on this day. The shofar recalls the shofar that was heard on Mount Sinai when the Torah was given. It reminds us that we heard G-d at Mount Sinai. It also recalls the ram that Abraham sacrificed instead of his son Isaac. It reminds us Isaac's bravery in doing G-d's will.

SPECIAL DAYS & PILGRIMAGES

Religious Studies GCSE: Judaism 1

YOM HAZIKARON

There are a number of customs associated with the night of Rosh Hashanah:

1. Before sundown, candles are lit as with every Shabbat and Yom Tov.

2. At the end of the evening service, besides the usual Yom Tov greeting, there is a special greeting formula to be recited in Hebrew. In English, it means: may you be inscribed and sealed immediately for a good and peaceful year. The reason for saying this is because the Talmud states that the completely righteous only have to recite one prayer on Rosh Hashanah (the evening prayer) and they are immediately inscribed in the book of life for the coming year.

3. After making Kiddush on wine and the blessing on the two challos, instead of dipping the pieces of challoh in salt as usual, they are dipped in honey. This is a symbol for a sweet new year. Some people continue dipping their bread in honey every day until Yom Kippur. Others continue until after the end of Sukkot. (It is also a custom to eat honey cake on Rosh Hashanah for the same reason.)

4. An apple is then taken and sliced and each piece is dipped in honey. Every person eats a slice. This symbolizes a sweet and fruitful year.

5. There are many other food customs which are meant to symbolize a good year ahead; the most widely practiced being to eat the head of a fish.

6. On the second night of Rosh Hashanah, at the beginning of the festive meal, there is a custom to eat a new fruit. This is because we need to make the shehecheyanu blessing in the Kiddush, but you cannot make this blessing twice for the same reason and we already made it on the first night. [In Jewish tradition, Rosh Hashanah is like one 48-hour day.] Someone who eats a new fruit, however, makes the shehecheyanu blessing on the fruit.

SPECIAL DAYS & PILGRIMAGES

Religious Studies GCSE: Judaism 1

ROSH HASHANAH MORNING

The prayer service of Rosh Hashanah is very long. It will start half an hour or an hour earlier than the usual Shabbat service and will finish about two hours longer than a normal Shabbat service. There are a number of practice associated with this service:

1. A special prayer book called a Machzor is used. Every Jewish festival has its own Machzor.

2. Many men have a custom to wear a kittel for the morning service. This is a white cloak/coat and is a symbol of purity. It is worn by a groom for his wedding ceremony for every bride and groom, if they repent on their wedding day, are forgiven all their sins. It is also worn for burial after the body has been immersed in a mikveh. It is worn to symbolize the purity we all hope to achieve through our prayers and repentance on Rosh Hashanah.

A kittel.

3. The morning (shacharit) and additional (mussaf) services are much longer than usual with many poems/songs called piyuttim added to the repetition of the Amidah. These piyuttim have very distinctive tunes and, for many people, it is the reciting of these piyuttim that gives the service its identity.

4. In between the two services the Torah portion is recited and then the first series of shofar notes are blown. Further series of shofar blowing takes place during the repetition of the Mussaf service. Chassidic communities blow the shofar during the silent Amidah as well.

SPECIAL DAYS & PILGRIMAGES

Religious Studies GCSE: Judaism 1

THE SHOFAR

The shofar is a hollowed-out ram's horn. One of the most important observances of this holiday is hearing the sounding of the shofar. A total of 100 notes are sounded both days. There are four different types of shofar notes:

tekiah - one sustained note;
shevarim - three short notes;
teruah – nine very short notes bown in very quick succession
shevarim-teruah – a combination of the two notes

The shevarim, teruah or shevarim-teruah are blown with a tekiah before and after. The length of the tekiah note varies so that it is always equal to the length of the middle note. The very last tekiah in each series is called a tekiah gedolah [big tekiah] and in some communities its note is extended much longer than all the others. If one of the days of Rosh Hashanah is Shabbat, the shofar is not blown.

TASHLICH

Another popular practice of the holiday is Tashlich, which means casting off. Everybody walks to where they can see flowing water, such as a stream or a river, on the afternoon of the first day. There is a prayer to be recited there and

then one's pockets are 'emptied' into the river, **symbolically casting off** all our sins. The practice of throwing small pieces of bread into the river is a mistake and actually might even violate the Yom Tov laws. Tashlich is normally observed on **the afternoon of the first day**, just after the afternoon (Minchah) service. When the first day occurs on Shabbat, tashlich is observed on the second day, because you need to carry your Machzor with you to say the tashlich prayer.

SPECIAL DAYS & PILGRIMAGES

Religious Studies GCSE: Judaism 1

QUESTION

(a) What is Rosh HaShanah? [1]

(b) Give two practices that Jews perform during the night of Rosh HaShanah. [2]

(c) Describe three practices associated with the day of Rosh HaShanah. [3]

(d) Explain how celebrating Rosh HaShanah affects the life of a Jew. [6]

(e) "All Jews should celebrate Rosh HaShanah." Discuss this statement. [12]

SPECIAL DAYS & PILGRIMAGES

Religious Studies GCSE: Judaism 1

YOM KIPPUR

SPECIAL DAYS & PILGRIMAGES

Religious Studies GCSE: Judaism 1

PREPARING FOR YOM KIPPUR

The days between Rosh Hashanah and Yom Kippur are called the Aseret Yemei Teshuvah which means the ten days of repentance. According to Orthodox Jewish tradition, everybody is judged on Rosh Hashanah. Those who are found to be completely righteous are inscribed in the Sefer HaChayim the book of life for a good year. Those who are found to be completely wicked are inscribed in the

Sefer HaMavet the book of death for a year of trouble, possibly for death. All those people who are neither righteous nor wicked are allotted these ten days to 'tip the scales' as judgement is suspended for them until Yom Kippur.

CUSTOMS FOR THE TEN DAYS OF REPENTANCE

There are a number of customs associated with these days:

1. Those who have not **ask forgiveness of others** before Rosh Hashanah will take more care to do so now.

2. When greeting people during Ellul, one traditionally says ketivah v'chatimah tovah may you be written and sealed for good. Between Rosh HaShanah and Yom Kippur this changes to gmar v'chatimah tovah may [it] be concluded and sealed for good.

3. It is appropriate to examine one's deeds more carefully now to see which mitzvoth one failed to observe properly in the previous year and to improve in the coming year, e.g. someone who regularly arrives late for prayers should be careful to be punctual at this time.

4. Three things in particular are said to be effective in removing a bad judgement: repentance, prayer and charity. One should therefore make efforts to be more charitable at this time and resolve to maintain this attitude in the coming year.

5. Although people go to work during this period, selichot are longer [most services start 45 minutes early] and some businesses will open later. Time is also set aside for more Torah study during these days.

6. Small additions and changes are made to the regular weekday services which focus attention on the themes of repentance and judgement.

SPECIAL DAYS & PILGRIMAGES

TZOM GEDALYAH – FAST OF GEDALIAH

The day after Rosh Hashanah is the fast of Gedaliah. After the Babylonians conquered Judea and destroyed the First Temple, they allowed a small remnant of the Jewish people to remain in Israel. They appointed the righteous **Gedaliah ben Achikam** as the Governor of Judea because they knew he only wanted to stay in Israel for religious reasons and he would not rebel against Babylonian rule. Sadly, the wicked **Ishmael ben Netanieh** was persuaded by the king of Ammon to assassinate Gedaliah and then join forces with Ammon to rebel against the Babylonians.

When the Babylonians heard what had happened they were so angry that the Governor they appointed had been killed that they drove all the remaining Jews out of the country. Gedaliah was assassinated on the day after Rosh Hashanah (some say it was actually on Rosh Hashanah) and that is why this day is observed as a half-day (sunrise to sunset) fast.

SHABBAT SHUVAH

This is the name for the Shabbat between Rosh Hashanah and Yom Kippur. It is considered the holiest Shabbat of the year. It is the custom in most Orthodox communities for the Rabbi to give a special Shabbat Shuvah address in the late afternoon which often lasts an hour or more. The theme of his address is always an aspect of repentance and, to accord dignity and seriousness to the occasion, the Rabbi usually wears his tallis to make the address.

Religious Studies GCSE: Judaism 1

EREV YOM KIPPUR

The Talmud comments that, when a person is on trial for their life, they do not help their case if they look guilty when they come into court! For this reason, as Yom Kippur approaches, the mood changes in a number of ways:

1. The early morning **selichot are very short**. A bare minimum is recited and it does not last more than 10-15 minutes.

2. It is a **mitzvah to eat** on Erev Yom Kippur. Many people have a plate of cakes and sweets arranged and whoever visits on that day is invited to eat something.

3. The Talmud describes a ritual called **kapparot**. Early in the morning, a live chicken is purchased and held above the head whilst reciting a declaration of atonement. The chicken slowly circles the head whilst the prayer is said. The chicken is then taken to be slaughtered and its meat is donated to the poor. **The Kapparot ceremony contains all three elements required to effect forgiveness: repentance, prayer and charity.** Nowadays, it is primarily Chassidim who maintain this custom. Other Orthodox Jews use money instead of a chicken and give the money to charity.

4. Men are accustomed to immerse in the **mikveh** to emphasise their commitment to purity in their actions.

5. A **festive meal**, which will include meat and wine, is eaten in the late afternoon as the final preparation for the fast.

SPECIAL DAYS & PILGRIMAGES

Religious Studies GCSE: Judaism 1

YOM KIPPUR

Yom Kippur, which falls on the **10th of Tishrei** is the most important festival of the Jewish year. Many Jews who do not observe any other Jewish customs will refrain from work, fast and/or attend synagogue services on this day. The name Yom Kippur means **Day of Atonement** and that pretty much explains what the holiday is. It is an entire day set aside to "afflict the soul," to atone for the sins of the past year.

LAWS AND CUSTOMS OF YOM KIPPUR

The following are just some of the most important laws and customs of this most holy of days:

1. Yom Kippur is comparable to Shabbat in that **all the restrictions of Shabbat apply** equally on Yom Kippur.

2. There are **five afflictions** that apply on Yom Kippur. One may not:
a) **eat or drink** from sunset until the following nightfall (about 25 hours)
b) **wash** any part of the body except the fingertips
c) use any **oils or lotions** to smooth the skin
d) **wear leather shoes** (no part of the shoe can contain leather)
e) engage in **marital relations.**

3. The entire day is spent in prayer. The evening service, called **Kol Nidrei,** lasts for one to two hours and many people remain in the synagogue afterwards, either studying Torah or reciting Psalms until they are ready to go to bed.

Some people even stay up the whole night. The morning service begins quite early and goes on until the mid-afternoon. There is then a short break until the afternoon and concluding service, called **Neilah** complete the day.

SPECIAL DAYS & PILGRIMAGES

Religious Studies GCSE: Judaism 1

4. One long note (a **tekiah gedolah**) is blown on the shofar to mark the end of the day. The regular evening service is then recited and the fast is broken by the **Havdalah** prayer over wine or grape-juice.

5. As on Rosh Hashanah, many men wear the **kittel** as a symbol of purity. This is a reminder of the promise made to Isaiah (which is recited in all the services of Rosh Hashanah, Yom Kippur and the Selichot) that if our sins be red as crimson they shall be made as white as snow.

6. Yom Kippur is the only day when men wear their **tallis** even at night. This is because Yom Kippur's five services are really one continuous 25-hour service. In some very observant communities there are no breaks between the services at all.

THE FIVE AFFLICTIONS

These five afflictions are intended to focus one's attention on the seriousness of the day:

FASTING is important because it's fun to eat and drink. Someone in a serious situation won't feel like eating. This law doesn't apply where a threat to life or health is involved. **Children under nine and women in childbirth are not permitted to fast**, even if they want to. Older children are permitted to fast, but may to break the fast if they feel the need to do so.

WASHING is also pleasurable. Soaking in a nice, hot bath or standing under a shower is very enjoyable. **Washing is only forbidden for pleasure**, not for cleanliness. If, for example, somebody got dirt on their face or arm, they would be permitted to wash it off with cold water.

OILS/LOTIONS are also **only forbidden for pleasure**. A sick person who is prescribed lotions may use them, even on Yom Kippur.

LEATHER SHOES used to be the most comfortable footwear. In the days of the Talmud, the only alternatives were wooden clogs or, for the very poor, foot coverings made of cloth. Trainers or synthetic slippers are just as comfortable as leather shoes today, but they are permitted. Wearing such footwear with one's best clothes is itself unusual and so the consciousness of the day is maintained even if the footwear is not so uncomfortable any more.

SPECIAL DAYS & PILGRIMAGES

MARITAL RELATIONS would be totally inappropriate on such a serious occasion. On Yom Kippur, Orthodox couples observe all the laws of separation that apply before a wife immerses in a mikveh.

THE FIVE SERVICES

The prayers for Yom Kippur are the most extensive and involved of the whole year. The evening service that begins Yom Kippur is commonly known as Kol Nidrei, named for the prayer that begins the service. Kol Nidrei means all vows and in this prayer, we ask G-d to annul all personal vows we may make in the coming year.

This prayer has often been cited by anti-Semites as proof that Jews are untrustworthy people who do not keep their vows. For this reason the Reform movement removed it from their Yom Kippur service for a while. In fact, the reverse is true: we make this prayer because we take vows so seriously that we consider ourselves bound even if we make the vows under duress or in times of stress when we are not thinking straight. This prayer gave comfort to those who were converted to Christianity by torture in various inquisitions, yet felt unable to break their vow to follow Christianity. The Reform movement later restored the prayer.

All five services on Yom Kippur have their own Amidah. At the end of each Amidah, both in the silent Amidah and in the Chazzan's repetition, a very important prayer called the viduy is added. Viduy means confession and this prayer includes a confession for every possible sin a person may have committed. All the confessions are written in the plural (we have sinned not I have sinned) to emphasise communal responsibility.

There are two basic parts of this confession: Ashamnu, a shorter, more general list (we have been treasonable, we have been aggressive, we have been slanderous...), and Al Cheit, a longer and more specific list (for the sin we sinned before you forcibly or willingly, and for the sin we sinned before you by acting callously...) Frequent petitions for forgiveness are interspersed in these prayers. There's also a catch-all confession: Forgive us the breach of positive commands and negative commands, whether or not they involve an act, whether or not they are known to us.. The Ashamnu prayer is also said at the end of the Selichot services but the Al Cheit is only recited on Yom Kippur.

SPECIAL DAYS & PILGRIMAGES

Religious Studies GCSE: Judaism 1

In the afternoon service, the book of Jonah is recited as the haftorah. This is because one of the central themes of this book is how Jonah disobeyed G-d's command but then saw the error of his ways, confessed his sins and repented sincerely. This is the example that every Jew is bidden to follow on Yom Kippur.

The concluding service of Yom Kippur, known as Ne'ilah, is unique to this day. The ark (where the Torah scrolls are kept) is left open throughout this service and so one should try to stand throughout the service. There is a tone of desperation in the prayers of this service. The service is sometimes referred to as the closing of the gates, the "last chance" to complete ones repentance before the holiday ends.

And finally….

After Yom Kippur ends, one should begin preparing for the next holiday, Sukkot, which begins five days later. There is a popular tradition to begin building the Sukkah on the night after Yom Kippur.

SPECIAL DAYS & PILGRIMAGES

Religious Studies GCSE: Judaism 1

QUESTION

(a) What do Jews call the days between Rosh HaShanah and Yom Kippur? [1]

(b) Give two customs that Jews follow during these days. [2]

(c) Describe three customs associated with the day before Yom Kippur. [3]

(d) Explain how observing Yom Kippur affects the life of a Jew. [6]

(e) "Yom Kippur is the most important day in the Jewish year." Discuss this statement. [12]

SPECIAL DAYS & PILGRIMAGES

Religious Studies GCSE: Judaism 1

PESACH

Pesach is a seven day (eight days outside Israel) holiday which marks the birth of the Jewish people It celebrates their liberation from slavery in Egypt over 3000 years ago. Pesach begins on the 15th Nisan. The English date varies from year to year, but it usually falls in April, occasionally at the end of March.

SPECIAL DAYS & PILGRIMAGES

Religious Studies GCSE: Judaism 1

PREPARING FOR PESACH

The Torah explains how, because the people had to leave Egypt in haste, they did not have time to allow their dough to rise. A major reminder of this is the prohibition against eating, having benefit from or even possessing **chametz** during Pesach.

WHAT IS CHAMETZ

Chametz is defined as **any fermented derivative of the five principal grains**, which are: wheat, oats, spelt, barley and rye. This includes obvious chametz products, such as bread, cake, biscuits, porridge oats, beer and whiskey. It also includes any foods that might be prepared with a mixture of chametz ingredients. Even the smallest amount of chametz is enough to prohibit the food for Pesach, e.g. fish balls are usually made with some kind of flour to bind them. If the flour is chametz, so are the fish balls.

Any pots, pans, cutlery and dishes that are used during the year with chametz also cannot be used on Pesach. This includes mixers, troughs and other implements used in food preparation. They too must be thoroughly cleaned and stored away until after Pesach.

SPECIAL DAYS & PILGRIMAGES

Religious Studies GCSE: Judaism 1

REMOVING THE CHAMETZ

Before Pesach, therefore, every Jew is required to remove all chametz from their home, other property and all premises under their jurisdiction, such as an office, locker or car. Even if one will not be on that premises during Pesach, as long as one is there within thirty days of Pesach, the obligation to remove all chametz before Pesach applies. These preparations for Pesach usually cover the entire thirty-day period that links Purim to Pesach. Slowly but surely, all chametz is removed from one's house (and other property) as it is even forbidden to own chametz on Pesach.

The home must be thoroughly cleaned of all chametz before Pesach. Any chametz that cannot be removed from a Jew's premises before Pesach must be discreetly stored away and sold to a non-Jew. Jewish law forbids the use of any chametz which remains in a Jew's possession during Pesach, even after the holiday is over.

Most people nowadays perform a legal ceremony which gives their local Rabbi the authority to sell their chametz on their behalf. This will be done during the week before Pesach and the Rabbi will conduct the sale with a non-Jew on Erev Pesach.

SEARCHING FOR CHAMETZ

Every Jew is required to make a thorough search in all places where chametz may have been kept or consumed any time during the previous year. The specified time for this search is Erev Pesach the night before Pesach, traditionally using a feather and the light of a single candle. The house should be clean by the time the search begins, as soon after nightfall as possible. The blessing on the removal of chametz is recited before the search begins, and a public disclaiming of ownership of chametz (called Bitul in Hebrew) is recited afterward.

SPECIAL DAYS & PILGRIMAGES

Religious Studies GCSE: Judaism 1

There is a kabbalistic custom to **hide ten pieces of chametz** (well wrapped up so that no crumbs slip out!) before the search begins. In many homes, whilst the men and boys go to Maariv (evening service) the women and girls hide the pieces. The men and boys will then have the task of finding them. Some say this also makes the search more diligent for, as the house will have been thoroughly cleaned by this time, in practice hardly any actual chametz is likely to be found.

FAST OF THE FIRST BORN

The day before Pesach is technically a fast day for Jewish firstborn males. **This is to recall the tenth plague, the slaying of all firstborn male Egyptians.** The fast recalls how the Jewish firstborn males were spared this plague. Some say that if a firstborn male is still too young to fast, his father (even if he is not a firstborn himself) must fast for him. **If Erev Pesach falls on Shabbat, the fast is brought forward to the previous Thursday.**

In practice, **firstborns rarely fast on this day**. Although the day is an official fast day, the Rabbis realized that, if firstborns were to fast, they would not be able to enjoy the Seder as they would be too hungry to discuss the redemption from Egypt and would be rushing to get to the meal as quickly as possible. For this reason, they provided a means for firstborns to be excused the fast. One who participates in a genuine seudat mitzvah is exempt from fasting. **In most communities, therefore, a Siyum (completion of a tractate of Talmud) is held at the end of the morning service**, following which a small 'meal' (usually cake and biscuits) is held. Participating firstborn males are then permitted to break their fast and eat normally for the rest of the day.

SPECIAL DAYS & PILGRIMAGES

Religious Studies GCSE: Judaism 1

BURNING THE CHAMETZ

The chametz that was found the previous evening will have been carefully stored away and, at the end of the morning, it is burned. **The burning of the chametz marks the end of any use of chametz** until after Pesach. In many homes a small bonfire is made which adds to the excitement and involvement of the children. After the chametz has been burnt another Bitul declaration is made, disclaiming ownership of any chametz one may have missed and failed to destroy. (If any chametz is actually found during Pesach it must be destroyed immediately.)

THE SPECIAL STATUS OF EREV PESACH

The afternoon of Erev Pesach has the status of Chol HaMoed (the intermediate days of Pesach). This is because, in the time of the Temple, the Paschal Lamb was brought to the Temple at this time for sacrifice. It was slaughtered in the Temple and its blood sprinkled on the Altar. It was then taken home to be roasted and eaten at the Seder. This is also the reason that all chametz has to be removed before the end of the morning of Erev Pesach.

SPECIAL DAYS & PILGRIMAGES

THE SEDER

The first night (first two nights outside Israel) of Pesach is called Seder night. The Seder follows a specific order as outlined in the Haggadah, the special 'siddur' composed for this night. A number of mitzvot are fulfilled during the course of the Seder:

MATZAH

We are commanded by Torah law to eat matzah during the Seder. There are two main reasons for this:

Matzah is a symbol of slavery. The Egyptians fed the Children of Israel (and probably all slaves) matzah, because it is an inferior food and also takes longer to digest, so they would not have to feed them so often.

Matzah is also a symbol of freedom. When G-d took us out of Egypt, He wished to teach us that He keeps His promises promptly, and therefore rushed us out of Egypt, without even giving us time to let our dough rise. We are therefore commanded to eat matzah on Seder night as a sign of the freedom attained on this night when we had to eat matzah.

Religious Studies GCSE: Judaism 1

SHEMURAH MATZOS

The best matzah to use for the Seder is shemurah matzah (guarded or protected matzos) made by hand. Immediately upon being harvested, the grain is guarded from moisture so that it does not become leavened. The grains are guarded from moisture at all times (even after it becomes flour) until it is finally matzah. These matzos are unlike the matzos you will find anywhere else, or any time else. They are specially made for Pesach. They look and taste unlike any other matzos. They are not usually baked square but round. They are much larger than ordinary matzos as well. (We will see the reason for this later.) For those who cannot eat wheat, shmuro matzos are also usually available in oat and spelt

MARROR

Marror means bitterness. We eat Marror because the Egyptians embittered the lives of our ancestors in Egypt. The purpose of the Marror, or bitter herbs, at the Seder is to remind us of the bitterness our ancestors (or we, ourselves, as we put ourselves in their place) were forced to suffer in Egyptian bondage. For this  reason, many people use grated horseradish and eat it along with other bitter herbs, such as romaine lettuce, endive, or iceberg lettuce. During the Seder, marror is eaten twice: once alone, and once with matzah, in a "sandwich". Although it was a Torah law to eat Marror in Temple times, now that we are unable to eat the Paschal Lamb (Korbon Pesach) it is a Rabbinic law nowadays.

TELLING YOUR CHILDREN THE STORY

The central mitzvah of the Seder involves the telling of the story of the redemption according to the order of the Haggadah. There is a specific section of the Haggadah called Maggid in which the story is told in a gradually more complex form. This is specifically designed with the participants in mind. Maggid begins with a simple explanation of the Exodus for the youngest present and then moves on to more difficult ideas to stimulate the older and more intelligent children.

SPECIAL DAYS & PILGRIMAGES

FOUR CUPS OF WINE

The Four Cups of wine drunk during the Seder recall the **four expressions of redemption** mentioned in the Torah at the time of the Exodus. They are:

(1) **I will take you out**
(2) **I will save you**
(3) **I will redeem you**
(4) **I will acquire you as a nation**

Since each of these cups of wine symbolise different aspects of redemption performed by G-d, a glass of wine is drunk at four different points in the Seder to acknowledge our appreciation for each stage. There is a fifth cup of wine called **The Cup of Elijah** and it is reserved for Elijah the Prophet, who is believed to visit each Seder that takes place around the world.

In the Torah, immediately after the four expressions of redemption, there is a fifth expression, I will bring you to the land. Does this mean we should drink five cups of wine? Most of the Rabbis understand this to refer to when we are brought permanently to the land in the days of the Messiah. The fifth cup is therefore poured out and left for Elijah to come and tell us whether the Messiah will come this year so that we can drink it. Until that happens, however, the fifth cup is not drunk.

Religious Studies GCSE: Judaism 1

THE SEDER PLATE

The Seder plate contains many of the food items that are essential for the Seder. The order of placing things on the Seder plate in this picture is the one followed by most families nowadays, but there are other customs followed as well.

SHANK BONE

A piece of roasted meat represents the lamb that was the korbon Pesach, the special Pesach sacrifice slaughtered on the eve of the redemption from Egypt and whose blood was smeared on the doorposts. In Temple times, the korbon Pesach was slaughtered in the Temple on the afternoon before Pesach, and eaten roasted at the end of the meal during the Seder.

ROASTED EGG

A hard-boiled egg is roasted to represent the korbon Chagigah, the holiday offering brought in the days of the Temple. The meat of this animal constituted the main part of the Pesach meal.

MARROR

Bitter herbs (maror) remind us of the bitterness of the slavery of our forefathers in Egypt. Fresh grated horseradish, romaine lettuce, and endive are the most common vegetables used. There are two slots for marror because it will be eaten twice at the Seder.

CHAROSET

Charoset is a mixture of apples, nuts, cinnamon and wine (some use dates as well) which resembles the mortar for bricks made by the Jews when they were slaves in Egypt.

SPECIAL DAYS & PILGRIMAGES

Religious Studies GCSE: Judaism 1

KARPAS

Karpas is a non-bitter vegetable. Many families use parsley. potato or carrot. This is a remembrance of the Temple when the laws of purity and impurity demanded that those who maintain a state of spiritual purity must wash their hands before eating wet vegetables.

Besides the Seder plate, two other essentials must be on the table before the Seder begins.

THREE MATZOT

Three matzot are placed on top of each other on a plate or napkin, and then covered. Most families have the custom to separate the matzot from each other with an interleaved holder for the matzot. It is possible to buy a Seder plate that contains three compartments underneath for the three matzot.

SALT WATER

A bowl of salt-water is necessary to dip in the karpas and also to dip in the hard-boiled egg with which the festive meal will begin.

Of course, plenty of wine is also needed for the four cups..........

SPECIAL DAYS & PILGRIMAGES

Religious Studies GCSE: Judaism 1

AN OUTLINE OF THE SEDER

The Seder contains **fifteen** sections:

1. KADESH
Every male over the age of Bar Mitzvah makes Kiddush and **the first cup of wine is drunk.**

2. URCHATZ
The leader of the Seder ritually washes his hands. (In some families all wash.) No blessing is made.

3. KARPAS
A non-bitter vegetable is dipped in salt-water and eaten. (One should be careful to eat less than the amount needed to make an after-blessing.)

4. YACHATZ
The middle matzah is broken. The smaller piece is returned and the larger piece is put aside to be eaten as the Afikomen. (In many families the children 'steal' the **Afikomen** and bargain for a present in exchange for its safe return!)

SPECIAL DAYS & PILGRIMAGES

5. MAGGID

The second cup of wine is poured and the youngest present asks the **Four Questions**. The story of the redemption from Egypt is then told. All are encouraged to contribute to the discussion (especially the children) but care should be taken not to take too long so that the younger children will be able to stay awake and enjoy the rest of the Seder. At the end of Maggid, **the second cup of wine is drunk.**

6. RACHTZAH

All ritually wash their hands (with a blessing) for the meal.

7. MOTZI

The three matzot are held by the leader of the Seder and he makes the blessing over bread.

8. MATZAH

The bottom matzah is put down and the blessing over the mitzvah to eat matzah is made. Everybody then eats a portion of matzah from the top two matzot.

9. MARROR

The marror is dipped in charoset (but the charoset is shaken off) and the blessing over the mitzvah to eat marror is made. **Everybody then eats the marror.**

10. KOREICH

A 'sandwich' is made using the bottom matzah and the marror. This is also dipped in charoset (but the charoset is shaken off) and a declaration is made that Hillel fulfilled the mitzvot of eating the korbon Pesach, the matzah and the marror all together. **The 'sandwich' is then eaten.**

Religious Studies GCSE: Judaism 1

11. SHULCHAN OREICH

The festive meal is now eaten. It is forbidden to eat roast meat during the meal in case it creates an impression that one has actually prepared a korbon Pesach which could only be eaten roasted. The meal traditionally begins with a boiled egg dipped in salt-water.

12. TZAFUN

The Afikoman (the larger part of the middle matzah broken at Yachatz) is now eaten as a reminder of the korbon Pesach, which was eaten at the end of the meal. (If the Afikoman had been 'stolen' by the children, the bargaining for presents takes place now!) It is forbidden to eat anything after the Afikoman in order that the taste of Pesach remains in our mouths the whole night.

13. BAREICH

The third cup of wine is poured and the Grace After Meals is recited. The third cup of wine is then drunk.

14. HALLEL

The fourth cup of wine is poured and the Hallel prayer is recited. It is a very joyous series of Psalms and many families sing the Hallel. The first two paragraphs are said before the meal, at the conclusion of Maggid and the rest is said now. The reason it is split up is because the first two paragraphs are about the Egyptian redemption, which is the theme of Maggid and the rest of Hallel is about the future Messianic redemption for which we now hope. Before beginning Hallel, the cup of Elijah is poured and the door is opened to welcome Elijah who, according to Jewish tradition, will come in advance of the Messiah to announce his imminent arrival. After Hallel is completed, the fourth cup of wine is drunk.

SPECIAL DAYS & PILGRIMAGES

Religious Studies GCSE: Judaism 1

15. NIRTZAH

We ask G-d to accept our Seder as a true expression of gratitude and appreciation for the redemption from Egypt. We also pray that the Messiah will arrive soon to complete our redemption so that we can all celebrate Pesach **next year in Jerusalem**. A number of traditional songs then complete the Seder, the last of which is **Chad Gadyah**, which sounds like a children's song but is actually a hint at the entire history of the Jewish People from the days of Jacob (who gave his father two goat-kids that his mother had prepared) until the final redemption and the revival of the dead.

After the Seder has finished, those with the strength and enthusiasm to do so will continue to discuss the redemption from Egypt through the night until sleep overtakes them............

SPECIAL DAYS & PILGRIMAGES

Religious Studies GCSE: Judaism 1

QUESTION

(a) Give another name for Pesach. [1]

(b) Name the two other pilgrim festivals. [2]

(c) State three things that happen on Pesach. [3]

(d) Explain why Pesach is an important festival for Jews. [6]

(e) "All Jewish festivals should be fun for children." Discuss this statement. [12]

SPECIAL DAYS & PILGRIMAGES

SHAVUOT

Shavuot is the festival which commemorates the giving of the Torah at Mount Sinai. In terms of status, it is equal to Pesach and Sukkot in that it is one of the three pilgrim festivals when all Jews would go up to the Temple. In practice, it is less special in the Jewish calendar, probably because it only lasts one day (two outside Israel) whilst Pesach and Sukkot are for a whole week.

Religious Studies GCSE: Judaism 1

THE DATE OF SHAVUOT

Shavuot has no specific date in the Torah. The Torah instructs us to count 49 days from the day after Pesach (the first day of Pesach, that is) and the 50th day is Shavuot. Now that the Jewish calendar has been fixed, however, **Shavuot always falls on 6 Sivan.**

SEFIRAT HA'OMER

The 49 days that link Pesach to Shavuot is counted as a form of elevation. When the Israelites came out of Egypt, they were at the lowest level of impurity and, in the 49 days between leaving Egypt and accepting the Torah, they elevated themselves through 49 levels of purity so they were worthy to stand at Mount

Sinai and hear G-d speak to them. **We also count these 49 days to elevate ourselves to be worthy to participate in Shavuot.** It is a Torah law to count the Omer.

CANNOT BEGIN BEFORE NIGHTFALL

Usually, a Shabbat or festival day can be started early. This demonstrates our enthusiasm for the day and is also very practical, especially in the summer when nightfall is quite late. **Shavuot, however, is the only festival that cannot begin early.** This is because of the Counting of the Omer. 49 complete days have to be counted before Shavuot and so the 49th day has to be completed before Shavuot can begin.

SPECIAL DAYS & PILGRIMAGES

Religious Studies GCSE: Judaism 1

CUSTOM: DECK THE SYNAGOGUE WITH FLOWERS

The Talmud says that Mount Sinai miraculously bloomed for the Israelites before the revelation. To commemorate this, it is a custom to bedeck the synagogue with flowers and to have extra flowers in one's home as well.

CUSTOM: STAY UP ALL NIGHT STUDYING TORAH

The Talmud also says that some of the Israelites overslept on the morning of Shavuot and were late for the revelation at Sinai! The custom has therefore arisen in many places to stay up all night on Shavuot and say the morning prayers at the earliest possible time. They usually start about 3.30-4.00 a.m. and finish about 6.00 a.m. Since the Torah reading for Shavuot includes the reciting of the Ten Commandments this is a kind of re-enacting of the revelation at Sinai.

AKDAMUS

This a special poem composed for Shavuot, that is recited before reading the Torah on the first day of Shavuot. It is written in Aramaic and each line ends with a word that ends in the Hebrew letters tav and aleph, which are respectively the last and the first letters of the Hebrew alphabet. This poetically symbolises the infinity of the Torah. It was written in the eleventh century by Rabbi Meir ben Yitzchok Nehorai. Akdamus is only said by Ashkenazim and not by Sephardim.

TEN COMMANDMENTS

The revelation at Mount Sinai was the most significant event in Jewish history. G-d Himself spoke the opening words of the Ten Commandments and all the people heard it. To commemorate this, the Torah reading on the first day includes the events leading up to the revelation and the recital of the Ten Commandments.

SPECIAL DAYS & PILGRIMAGES

Religious Studies GCSE: Judaism 1

MEGILLAT RUTH

Every festival is marked by a Megillah recital. Outside Israel, this is recited on the second day. The book of Ruth is read on Shavuot because of its message concerning commitment to G-d and the Torah. Ruth is the most obvious example of overcoming hardship for the sake of observing the Torah. She was a Moabite princess who gave up status, wealth and security to live a life of poverty, rejection and loneliness because of her commitment  to the Torah. On the festival when all Jews are supposed to renew their own personal commitment to the Torah, one is inspired by the example of Ruth.

CUSTOM: EAT CHEESE CAKE

The Talmud states that, when the Israelites heard the kashrut laws, they realised that they did not know how to prepare meat properly and so, on the first Shavuot, everybody ate dairy. To recall this, there is a widespread custom to eat dairy foods during the festival and in most communities cheese-cake is an acknowledged Shavuot delicacy nowadays.

SPECIAL DAYS & PILGRIMAGES

QUESTION

(a) Give another name for Shavuot. [1]

(b) Name the two other pilgrim festivals. [2]

(c) State three things that happen on Shavuot. [3]

(d) Explain why Shavuot is an important festival for Jews. [6]

(e) "Shavuot is not as important as the other festivals." Discuss this statement. [12]

Religious Studies GCSE: Judaism 1

SUKKOT

Sukkot is the last of the Shalosh Regalim (the three pilgrimage festivals). Like Pesach and Shavuot, Sukkot has both a historical and an agricultural significance. Historically, Sukkot commemorates the forty-year period during which the children of Israel were wandering in the desert, living in temporary dwellings. Agriculturally, Sukkot is a harvest festival. It falls at the conclusion of the ingathering of the harvest and for that reason is called Chag HaAsif, which means festival of ingathering.

SPECIAL DAYS & PILGRIMAGES

Religious Studies GCSE: Judaism 1

PREPARING FOR SUKKOT

Sukkot is the most joyous of all the Jewish festivals and is called **Zman Simchateinu,** which mans the time of our rejoicing. It begins on the 15th Tishrei, just five days after Yom Kippur. Immediately after Yom Kippur finishes, everybody gets busy **building a Sukkah** and buying **Arba Minim** (the four species) which are waved every morning of Sukkot (except Shabbat).

SPECIAL DAYS & PILGRIMAGES

Religious Studies GCSE: Judaism 1

Sukkot lasts for seven days. The first two days (only the first in Israel) are **Yom Tov** on which work is not done. The other days are called **Chol HaMoed** which is untranslatable in English. It means literally ordinary festival days. In practice, it means that they are festive days but work is permitted on them if necessary. Sukkot is followed immediately by the festival of **Shemini Atzeret/Simchat Torah** which lasts one day in Israel and two everywhere else. Technically, this is a separate holiday but it is related to Sukkot. In many ways it represents the conclusion of Sukkot.

LAWS CONCERNING THE SUKKAH

The word Sukkot means literally booths or huts and refers to the temporary dwellings that are erected as a remembrance for period of wandering in the wilderness. The word sukkah is the singular form of the word sukkot. **Since this is the name of the festival, this is a reason why some might say the Sukkah was the most important mitzvah associated with this festival.**

SPECIAL DAYS & PILGRIMAGES

Religious Studies GCSE: Judaism 1

1. A Sukkah must have **at least two and a half walls** covered with a material that will not blow away in the wind. Why two and a half walls? According to Jewish tradition, this was one of the oral laws taught at Mount Sinai. The Hebrew letters of the word Sukkah hint at this law as well: the samech has four sides, the kof has three sides and the hei has two and a half sides.

2. The walls of the Sukkah do not have to be solid; canvas covering tied or nailed down is acceptable and quite common in many places. The walls must be secure enough, however, that **they will not blow down in a normal wind** for that locality.

3. **A Sukkah may be any size**, so long as it is large enough to fulfill the commandment of dwelling in it. (The Mishnah gives a minimum size of seven square handbreadths; a handbreadth is about three inches.)

4. The roof of the Sukkah is the most important part of the whole structure. It must be made of material referred to as **sechach** which means covering. The laws of what can be used for sechach are very strict. It must be something that **grew from the ground** but has now been **completely detached**, such as tree branches, straw or bamboo poles.

5. Sechach must be **left loose**, not tied together or tied down.

6. Sechach should be thick but not too thick. Preferably, it should be sparse enough that **the stars can be seen**. It must be dense enough, however, that it does not provide more light than shade.

7. **The Sukkah must be made first** and the sechach only put on when it is finished.

8. In temperate countries like in England, most people prepare **a water-proof cover** over the top of the Sukkah when it is raining to protect the contents of the Sukkah, but the Sukkah cannot be used while it is covered.

9. The commandment to dwell in a Sukkah can be fulfilled by simply **eating all of one's meals there**. If the weather, climate, and one's health permit, however, one should spend as much time in the Sukkah as possible, even sleeping there.

SPECIAL DAYS & PILGRIMAGES

Religious Studies GCSE: Judaism 1

It is considered a hiddur mitzvah (beautifying the mitzvah) to decorate the Sukkah. It is quite common to **put up posters with Sukkot themes**, pictures of famous Rabbis or images of the Temple service. Many people also **hang fruit** from the sechach. Some people even put up streamers and other festive decorations.

LAWS CONCERNING THE ARBA MINIM

Another important feature of Sukkot involves what are known as the Four Species (arba minim in Hebrew). We are commanded to take these four plants and use them to rejoice before G-d.

Religious Studies GCSE: Judaism 1

1. The four species in questions are:

- an etrog (a citrus fruit similar to a lemon; in English it is called a citron);

- a palm branch (in Hebrew, lulav);

- three myrtle branches (hadassim);

- two willow branches (aravot).

2. The six branches are all bound together and referred to collectively as the lulav, because the palm branch is by far the largest part. The etrog is held separately.

3. With these four species in hand, one recites the blessing and waves the species in all six directions (east, south, west, north, up and down) symbolizing the fact that G-d is ruler everywhere.

4. The Arba Minim are also held during Hallel, the series of joyous Psalms recited on all three pilgrim festivals, and they are waved again at specific points in the recital.

5. The Arba Minim are also held again during the Hoshana prayer, when all the men circuit the bimah at the end of the Shacharit service each day of Sukkot.

6. On the seventh day of Sukkot, seven circuits are made during the Hoshana recital. For this reason, the seventh day of Sukkot is known as Hoshana Rabbah, which means literally the great Hoshana.

SPECIAL DAYS & PILGRIMAGES

Religious Studies GCSE: Judaism 1

LAWS CONCERNING THE HOSHANA RECITALS

These recitals connect Sukkot to Rosh Hashanah and Yom Kippur. The Talmud states that although the judgement is written on Rosh Hashanah and sealed on Yom Kippur, the book is not closed until Hoshana Rabbah. After we have expressed our willingness to 'do better' in the coming year, we are given a festival with so many different mitzvot to perform. By observing Sukkot properly, we merit that the good judgement for which we were sealed on Yom Kippur should remain for us:

1. In the Temple, the kohanim used to take a giant aravah (willow branch) every day of Sukkot and make a circuit around the sacrificial altar. On Hoshana Rabba they circuited the altar seven times.

2. The aravah symbolizes our unworthiness and dependence on G-d's forgiveness.

3. We recall this ceremony nowadays by circuiting the bimah every morning of Suukkot with the arba minim.

4. The word Hoshana (which begins and ends every line of the recital made during the circuit) means please save (us). We acknowledge the need for G-d's forgiveness.

5. On Hoshana Rabbah, many people stay up all night to learn Torah. There is a tradition in many communities to recite the entire book of Deuteronomy on the night of Hoshana Rabbah.

6. When we circuit the bimah seven times in the morning, it is comparable to the story of Joshua in Jericho. There, they circuited the walls once every day and on the seventh day they circuited seven times and then the walls fell down and the Israelites captured the city.

7. After the seven circuits, we take a specially prepared bunch of aravos and beat them on the ground, symbolizing the destruction of all our sins.

SPECIAL DAYS & PILGRIMAGES

LAWS CONCERNING SHEMINI ATZERET

The festival of Shemini Atzeret follows immediately after Sukkot. Many people mistakenly refer to it as the last day of Sukkot, but it is a different festival with its own laws:

1. Now that Sukkot is over (and we are not living in the Sukkah any more) our attention turns to winter and we say a special prayer for rain (tefillat geshem) on Shmini Atzeret morning.

2. In Israel, Shemini Atzeret is one day. Outside Israel, on the second day, the Rabbinic festival of Simchat Torah is celebrated. (In Israel, everything happens on one day.) On this day, the annual reading of the Torah is completed and started again.

3. This is an extremely joyous occasion and much singing and dancing accompanies this celebration, in some communities going on for many hours.

4. It is a special honour to be called up for the reading of the last portion of the Torah. The person called up is called the Chatan Torah which means the bridegroom of the Torah.

5. Immediately after the Torah is completed it is begun again. The person given the honour of being called up for the reading of the beginning of the Torah is called the Chatan Bereishis which means the bridegroom of the beginning.

6. After the service, in many communities the festive meal of the day is eaten by everybody together in the synagogue amidst great joy. It is the happiest communal celebration of the entire Jewish year.

SPECIAL DAYS & PILGRIMAGES

Religious Studies GCSE: Judaism 1

NOTE: THE SIGNIFICANCE OF ARBA MINIM

Why are these four plants used instead of other plants? There are two primary explanations of the symbolic significance of these plants:

They represent different parts of the human body

The long straight lulav represents the spine.

The hadassim, which are small and oval in shape, represents the eye.

The aravah, a long oval, represents the mouth.

The etrog fruit represents the heart.

These parts of the body are the most susceptible to be used for sin, but should join together in the performance of mitzvot.

They represent different types of Jews

The etrog has both a pleasing taste and a pleasing scent. It represents those Jews who have achieved both knowledge of Torah and performance of mitzvot.

The hadassim, which have a strong scent but no taste, represent Jews who perform mitzvot but have little knowledge of Torah.

The lulav, which produces tasty fruit, but has no scent, represents Jews who have knowledge of Torah but are lacking in mitzvot.

The aravot, which have neither taste nor scent, represent Jews who have no knowledge of Torah and do not perform the mitzvot.

We bring all four of these species together on Sukkot to remind us that every Jew is important and we have to strive for greater unity among ourselves.

SPECIAL DAYS & PILGRIMAGES

Religious Studies GCSE: Judaism 1

QUESTION

(a) What is a Sukkah? [1]

(b) Name two of the Four Species (Arba Minim). [2]

(c) Describe three other practices associated with the festival of Sukkot. [3]

(d) Explain how celebrating Sukkot affects the life of a Jew. [6]

(e) "Living in a hut is a funny way to worship G-d." Discuss this statement. [12]

SPECIAL DAYS & PILGRIMAGES

MAJOR DIVISIONS AND INTERPRETATIONS

Religious Studies GCSE: Judaism 1

INTRODUCTION

Following the destruction of the Temple and the expulsion of Jews from the land of Israel, first by the Babylonians and then by the Romans, the Jewish communities of Babylonia became the centre of Jewish life for approximately 1000 years. It was there that the Talmud was compiled and almost all of the major Jewish scholars lived.

When these communities began to break down in the eleventh century, the Jewish world became divided into those communities which settled in Northern Europe and became known as Ashkenazim and those which remained in the Middle East or North Africa and were later known as Sephardim (or Oriental Jews). Although Ashkenazim and Sephardim may appear to be very different, their core beliefs are very similar. Their main differences are cultural or environmental and a consequence of their living in different parts of the world. Both Ashkenazim and Sephardim would be included in what would later be called Orthodox Judaism.

The most noticeable differences between Ashkenazim and Sephardim are:

they pronounce Hebrew differently

their style of dress is different

they have different customs regarding special foods on Shabbat and festivals

Since the Second World War, especially in Israel, Ashkenazim and Sephardim have become much more similar and many of these differences are becoming less noticeable.

MAJOR DIVISIONS & INTERPRETATIONS

Religious Studies GCSE: Judaism 1

ORTHODOX JUDAISM

The word Orthodox (from the Latin, meaning literally correct belief) was first used by a nineteenth century Reform writer who intended it to be a derogatory description of those who stuck to the 'old fashioned ways' in much the same way that the term Ultra-Orthodox is used today to describe religious Jews who appear to live in their own closed-off societies. In time, however, the label stuck and by the mid-twentieth century had ceased to have a derogatory connotation.

The word Orthodox has now become the acceptable identification of those Jews who believe that the Torah was given by G-d at Mount Sinai. Before the nineteenth century, however, there were no alternative Jewish identities to that which is now labelled Orthodox. A Jew was either 'part of the faith' or someone who lived completely outside the Jewish community and soon ceased to be identified as a Jew at all.

Today, Orthodox Judaism is made up of different groups who, although having the same fundamental beliefs in G-d and the Torah and observing the same mitzvoth, both from the Torah and from the Rabbis, are very different in their attitude to how Judaism is to be lived. The most identifiable groupings, are:

Chareidim   Modern Orthodox

Chassidim   Religious Zionist

Both Ashkenazim and Sephardim can be found in all these groups.

MAJOR DIVISIONS & INTERPRETATIONS

Religious Studies GCSE: Judaism 1

CHAREIDIM

Chareidim are what remains of the 'original' Orthodox Jews before the other groups broke away to form their own identities. They are easily identifiable by their style of dress: **men wear predominantly black suits and black trilby-styled hats** whilst women's fashions will emphasise the principles of modesty. **Chareidim strongly encourage Yeshivah** education for boys after school. Many remain in full-time study until after they are married.

The major Chareidi communities are:

Jerusalem and **Bnei Brak** in Israel
Brooklyn and **Monsey** in New York
Golders Green, **Manchester** and **Gateshead** in England.

There are many more Chareidi communities all over the world, but these are the main Chariedi centres today. In Israel, Chareidim have formed their own political parties and have a small number of seats in the Knesset, the Israeli parliament. Bnei Brak even has Chareidi Mayor.

MAJOR DIVISIONS & INTERPRETATIONS

Religious Studies GCSE: Judaism 1

CHASSIDIM

The Chassidic movement began in Poland in the eighteenth century. It was a response to the terrible persecutions that afflicted that part of the world at that time. Slanderous, anti-Semitic leaflets and articles became more and more common, Jews were routinely accused of ritual murder and peasant mobs were regularly incited to commit pogroms. Jews were banned from the professions, from political involvement or from owning land. Special 'Jew-taxes' were enacted and enormous rents charged by Polish landowners in the villages and small rural townlets where Jews were permitted to live.

Large numbers of Jews became isolated from Torah study or genuine Rabbinic leadership. Those who lived in outlying villages often did not even have ten adult males to make their own minyan and lacked schools for their children. Ignorance was becoming more common and there was a complete lack of spiritual elevation. The crippling poverty and despair threatened to completely demoralise Polish Jewry. There was a great risk that large numbers of Jews would simply give up the struggle to maintain a Jewish identity, so strong were the forces that were lined up against them. It was in response to this potential tragedy that Chassidut emerged.

MAJOR DIVISIONS & INTERPRETATIONS

THE BA'AL SHEM TOV

Yisrael ben Eliezer was born in 1700 (some say 1698) and was orphaned at an early age. As a child, he soon became aware of the poverty and despair of his fellow Jews. Many legends abound concerning his early life, working first as a labourer and later as a Shochet (ritual slaughterer) and travelling from town to town trying to comfort and encourage the poor and downtrodden communities he found. By the age of 36, a group of disciples had formed around this unusual 'holy man' with new ideas about the nature of holiness and spirituality.

In those days, the world of the Yeshivah was closed to all but the greatest scholars. Its students were extremely pious intellectual giants who would be the leaders of the next generation. In good times, people would draw inspiration from the Yeshivah scholars and every family would struggle to send at least one son to study whilst the rest of the family worked to support him. Scholarship had always been the identifying characteristic of a 'good' Jew. Each family had its scholar who would inspire them to redouble their efforts in Torah study.

In eighteenth century Poland, however, Yeshivah study was a luxury that very few could afford. This was having a calamitous effect on communal life. If there were no scholars around, how could a person be a good Jew? The Ba'al Shem Tov had a revolutionary solution to this problem.

The Ba'al Shem Tov suggested that there could be an alternative religious expression to Torah study. He taught that an ordinary unlearned Jew could also achieve the highest spiritual levels even if he was not a Torah scholar. He could achieve this by devotion in prayer, by a meticulous concern for the details of simple everyday commandments and by actively seeking out simple acts of piety, kindness and generosity of spirit to others. The word Chassid means literally pious one and the Chasidic movement promotes integrating piety into daily life.

Religious Studies GCSE: Judaism 1

THE DEVELOPMENT OF CHASSIDUT

Within two generations, Chassidut had expanded throughout Poland as the students of the Baal Shem Tov spread his message far and wide. Each village or shtetel established its own Chassidic 'branch' with its own Rebbe or leader. In time, each branch developed its own customs, practices and styles of dress.

The role of the Rebbe was absolutely crucial to the development of Chassidut. Often, he was the only person in the village who was a Torah scholar and he was revered by his followers as almost superhuman. His rulings would be sought for even the most basic of problems and his pronouncements were never challenged.

Throughout the nineteenth century, the Chassidic movement succeeded in providing a secure and meaningful Jewish identity for the masses of unlearned Jews in Poland. When the Nazi Holocaust wiped out Polish Jewry completely, so strong was the Chassidic identity that Polish villages 'regrouped' in Israel and America as Rebbes escaped or new Rebbes were appointed.

To this day, Polish villages such as Bobov, Viznitz, Lubavitch, Ger, Breslau, Satmar and Belz are still identifiable as Chassidic groupings.

MAJOR DIVISIONS & INTERPRETATIONS

CHASSIDUT TODAY

Chassidim are also easily identifiable by their style of dress: men wear long black silk coat/jackets and many retain the dress styles of the orginal Polish communities. Their black hats are a distinctive circular style and on Shabbat and festival they were special round fur hats called shtreimels.  Many Chassidic women will wear a special head-covering called a tichel rather than the wigs worn by other Orthodox married women. Chassidim minimize secular education for their children and are strongly opposed to university education as they fear the social environment there will be very corrupting.

The major Chassidic communities are in:

Meah Shearim (Jerusalem) and Safed in Israel
Williamsburg, Monroe and Boro Park in New York
Stamford Hill in England.

 One Chassidic group, known as Lubavitch or Chabad, is committed to outreach programmes. They strive to influence non-Orthodox Jews to become more observant. Chabad have centres all over the world and, in many places, they are the only Orthodox programme available. In 2008, the Chabad centre in Mumbai was targeted by terrorists and its leaders were murdered.

Religious Studies GCSE: Judaism 1

MODERN ORTHODOX

Throughout the nineteenth century, particularly in Germany, the Reform movement presented a major challenge to mainstream Orthodox Jewish life. (See below for an explanation of Reform Judaism.) In the second half of the nineteenth century, a new Orthodox movement began in Germany as a response to Reform. Due to the fact that it was 'new' it became known as the Neo-Orthodox movement (neo is Latin for new). Today this movement is usually called Modern Orthodox.

The founder of Modern Orthodox Judaism was Rabbi Samson Raphael Hirsch, the Chief Rabbi of Frankfurt and one of the outstanding Orthodox scholars of his generation. He committed himself to demonstrating that it was not necessary to join the Reform movement to be a 'modern' Jew.

At first, Hirsch's ideas were considered very controversial among other Orthodox leaders:

> He spoke and wrote in German rather than in Yiddish or Hebrew
>
> He wore Western dress styles although, of course, did not compromise on matters of modesty.
>
> He also encouraged secular education for children and was himself proficient in many secular subjects.

MAJOR DIVISIONS & INTERPRETATIONS

Hirsch attacked Reform Judaism on every issue and both his major works, **Horeb** (a philosophical analysis of the commandments) and his **Commentary on the Torah** were critical of Reform ideas. He did not believe that Reform leaders were wicked, but that they were misguided. Whilst well-intentioned, Reform would ultimately be just a stepping-stone on the path to assimilation.

Hirsch also popularised the Mishnaic slogan: **Torah Im Derech Eretz**. He explained this to mean that any secular area of study (derech eretz) which enhances one's knowledge of Torah is a legitimate area of study. In his commentary on the Torah, he compares the lights of the Menorah to different 'branches' of study, studying (like candles) being the 'illumination' of the world. Just as there was a central stem on the Menorah and all the other branches leaned towards it, so is the study of Torah the 'central stem' of every Jew's learning, and all the other academic disciplines, as it were, lean towards it to further illuminate its message.

The mainstream Orthodox world soon realised that Hirsch was one of their champions and his neo-Orthodox revolution soon became an accepted part of Orthodoxy, apart from within the Chassidic world.

MODERN ORTHODOXY TODAY

Modern Orthodox Jews will typically wear western-styles clothes and, apart from their kippot and the women not wearing trousers, are indistinguishable from mainstream dress culture. Modern Orthodox culture **encourages university education** and there are even some Modern Orthodox universities:

> **Bar Ilan** in Israel
> **Yeshiva University** in New York
> **the London School of Jewish Studies** in London.

Although it is not specifically a part of Modern Orthodox ideology, **most Modern Orthodox Jews identify strongly with Zionism and the State of Israel.**

Religious Studies GCSE: Judaism 1

RELIGIOUS ZIONISM

The land of Israel has always been central to Judaism. In the Torah, when He chose Abraham to be the first Jew, G-d promised the land to Abraham's descendants for an eternal possession.

Even though the Jews were exiled, first by the Babylonians and then by the Romans, Jeremiah prophesised that the exile would eventually end and Israel would return at the end of days when G-d would enter into a new covenant with them.

Religious Zionists are those who believe that the re-establishing of a Jewish state in the Holy Land signals the beginning of the end of the exile.

MAJOR DIVISIONS & INTERPRETATIONS

MODERN ZIONISM

Modern Zionism is political movement that began in the nineteenth century in Tsarist Russia. It was one of the responses to the extremely harsh persecutions endured by Jews at that time.

Many Jews discarded their religion in their despair and joined other persecuted people in trying to resist the Tsarist tyranny. They became influenced by the national movements that arose throughout Eastern Europe at this time and the idea soon developed that a national home for Jews would be a 'solution' to the Jewish Problem.

The early Zionists were anti-religious and believed a Jewish state would mean that religion was no longer necessary to maintain a Jewish identity. Not surprisingly, the religious leaders were strongly opposed to Zionism at first.

By the end of the nineteenth century, however, many religious Jews started to interpret the growing movement for a Jewish state as the fulfilment of Jeremiah's prophecy that the exile would eventually come to an end.

Rabbi Abraham Isaac Kook encouraged support for Zionism and spread the belief that, by going to live in Israel and helping to rebuild the land, Jews were bringing the Messianic Age closer.

Religious Studies GCSE: Judaism 1

ZIONISM IN THE TWENTIETH CENTURY

The Zionist movement made great progress in the early years of the twentieth century. Its first significant leader was Theodore Herzl. Herzl was an assimilated Viennese Jew who worked as a journalist. Whilst in France covering the trial of a Jew called Dreyfus who had been arrested on trumped up charges of treason, he witnessed the French mobs screaming "Death to Dreyfus, death to the Jews".

Herzl was shocked by the sight and he became convinced of the need to fight against anti-Semitism. At first, he wanted to take all the Jews to the Vatican where they could all be converted to Catholicism and so end the Jewish problem!

After realising that this was impractical, Herzl decided that the only way to deal with anti-Semitism was to give Jews their own homeland. He developed his ideas in a book called The Jewish State and in another volume Altneuland, he set out his vision for that country.

Herzl spent the rest of his life promoting the ideas of a Jewish state, but was not concerned where it would be. When a suggestion was made that a Jewish state be created in Uganda, he was strongly in favour and only the objections of the Religious Zionists stopped it from happening.

Herzl believed that his mission was to normalise the Jewish people. Once they were like the other nations with their own land, he believed, Jews would cease to be persecuted.

Herzl died in 1905. His picture hangs above the seat of the Speaker of the Knesset. He is buried in Jerusalem in a special tomb on a mountain that has been renamed Mount Herzl.

MAJOR DIVISIONS & INTERPRETATIONS

His is a very different idea to the one promoted by Rav Kook, the founder of Religious Zionism. **Rav Kook believed that the settlement of the Land of Israel is a major religious duty,** which should be celebrated. His vision was to create a state of Israel where traditional Judaism would be renewed and people would feel more connected to G-d and to the principles of Judaism. He felt that **by living in Israel Jews would be able to live religious lives which were more creative than they were in the Diaspora.** As a counter to the secular Zionist youth movements that emerged at this time, **Bnei Akiva**, a religious youth movement, was formed to promote a religious identification with the land of Israel.

THE CREATION OF THE STATE

A number of historical factors lead to the creation of the state of Israel:

The collapse of the Ottoman Empire. During the First World War (1914-18) the Turkish Ottoman empire, which had ruled most of Middle East for over 400 years, disintegrated. **The Holy Land came under the control of Britain.**

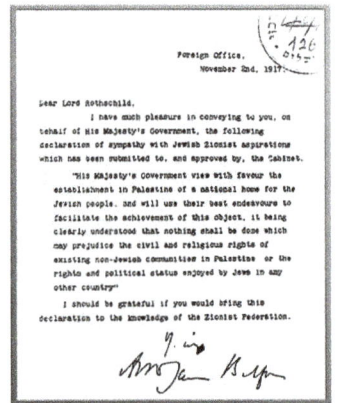

The Balfour Declaration. In 1917, the English Foreign Secretary, Lord Balfour, issued a declaration ensuring a Jewish homeland be established in the territories under its Mandate. The borders of this homeland were not defined and have always been a matter of dispute with the new Arab states of Jordan and Syria which also received their independence at this time.

The Nazi Holocaust. Throughout the 1920's and 1930's there was a steady growth of Jewish immigration (aliyah) both of religious and secular Zionists. The Holocaust, however, created an urgent need for a haven from persecution and completely changed the attitudes of Jews all over the world to Zionism. Before the Holocaust, many Orthodox Jews were suspicious that Zionism was

an anti-religious movement and did not support it. Religious Zionists were a small minority. By the time the full impact of the Holocaust was realized, however, almost all Jews supported the move for the creation of a Jewish State to ensure that nothing like this could ever happen again. Only a few Chassidic groups (most notably Satmer Chassidim) continued to oppose Zionism.

Religious Studies GCSE: Judaism 1

RELIGIOUS ZIONISM TODAY

For Religious Zionists, living in Israel and promoting the ideal of other Jews living in Israel is the central religious issue. Religious Zionism has its own Yeshivot and its own Kibbutzim. It believes in making Zionists more religious and religious people more Zionistic. Many Modern Orthodox Jews support the ideas of Religious Zionists, Chareidim tend to be more ambivalent and Chassidim tend to be more anti-Zionist.

MAJOR DIVISIONS & INTERPRETATIONS

Religious Studies GCSE: Judaism 1

REFORM JUDAISM

Reform Judaism is a movement that began in Germany in the early nineteenth century. It was the first 'version' of Judaism in almost 2000 years of Jewish history that did not accept as a central principle of belief that G-d gave the Torah to Israel at Mount Sinai.

There was a big change in political outlook in Western Europe after the French Revolution (1789). Many countries extended new freedoms and rights to minorities previously considered to be second-class citizens. This period came to be known as the Age of Enlightenment. Jews also benefited from these changes, especially in Germany.

The advantages of enlightenment, however, also came with a feeling of trying to be more accommodating of German ways. The first Reform synagogues were made to look more 'German' in an open society.

MAJOR DIVISIONS & INTERPRETATIONS

Religious Studies GCSE: Judaism 1

The first Reform service was held in Seesen, Westphalia led by Israel Jacobson:

> He introduced sermons into the service, given in German instead of Yiddish
> He also introduced an organ into the synagogue
> He also emphasised decorum during prayers.

The first Reform Synagogue (they called it a Temple to differentiate it from Orthodox places of worship) was opened in Hamburg in 1819. In the same year the first Reform Siddur (prayer book) was produced. It removed all references to Zion and the rebuilding of the Temple. This was to display the fact that they were committed German citizens with no conflicting loyalties. In the second generation of Reform, they distanced themselves even further from Orthodox Judaism.

Abraham Geiger (1810-1874) promoted the idea that humans had been involved in the writing of the Torah. This led to his theory of Progressive Revelation which states that each generation could decide how Judaism should develop, which mitzvot were no longer relevant and which new mitzvot were needed. He explained Messianic hope as an age of universal peace which would be brought about by the Age of Enlightenment, rather than by the Jewish return to Israel.

His colleague, Samuel Holdhem (1806-1860) went even further. He abolished

> Circumcision,
> Wearing a kippa or tallit
> Blowing shofar
> Using the Hebrew language.
> He denied any connection of German Jews with the land of Israel
> He moved Shabbat from Saturday to Sunday.

Throughout the nineteenth century, Reform Judaism saw itself as modern Judaism for the future which the Age of Enlightenment had begun. Orthodox Judaism, by contrast, was the Judaism of the past, the Judaism of the ghetto and the medieval world. Since the Age of Enlightenment would bring an end to persecution, the new Zionist movement was also unnecessary. Reform continued to oppose Zionism until the Nazi era.

MAJOR DIVISIONS & INTERPRETATIONS

Religious Studies GCSE: Judaism 1

REFORM TODAY

Reform Judaism today is far more traditional than it was in the nineteenth century. Its services are much more similar to Orthodox services, Shabbat has returned to Saturday and Reform is now a strong supporter of Zionism.

In some ways, however, the outlook of Reform is very similar to what it was in Germany. **It still sees itself as the 'modern' voice of Judaism.** It promotes modern causes such as the equality of women (ordaining women as Rabbis), accepting homosexuality and promoting 'progressive' issues such as environmental protection, animal welfare and inter-faith dialogue.

MAJOR DIVISIONS & INTERPRETATIONS

Religious Studies GCSE: Judaism 1

LIBERAL JUDAISM

Liberal Judaism is a more progressive version of Judaism than Reform. It was founded in the early twentieth century by Lily Montagu (1873-1963) and Claude Montefiore (1858-1938) a passionate anti-Zionist who believed in combining what he believed were the best elements of Judaism and Christianity. He suggested that both Jesus and St. Paul should  be considered religious authorities who 'modernised' the Judaism of their time. Possibly, he considered Christianity to be the Liberal Judaism of 2000 years ago.

The first Liberal service was held in 1902. It aimed to use more English in its services than the Reform, permit men and women to sit together, use organ accompaniment and provide a more inclusive environment that would be more attractive to those Jews uninspired by traditional synagogue services. The first Liberal synagogue was opened in 1911 and today there are over thirty Liberal synagogues in Great Britain.

The modern Liberal movement, however, whilst rejecting the specifics of Montefiore's ideas, continue to promote his general principle of combining the best of modern scholarship with a focus on the ethical rather than the legal content of Jewish teachings. Examples of their more progressive attitude than the Reform include their acceptance of a child of a Jewish father as being Jewish even if his mother is not Jewish. Also, they permit same-sex marriages.

MAJOR DIVISIONS & INTERPRETATIONS

Now fervently pro-Zionist, in 1979 they also established a Zionist youth movement called **Netzer**, which stands for **Noar Tzioni Reformi** ('Reform Zionist Youth'). This name was changed in 1996 by the Australian movement to Noar Tzioni Mitkademet ('Progressive Zionist Youth')

DIFFERENCES BETWEEN ORTHODOX AND REFORM JUDAISM

ORTHODOX	REFORM
The Torah was given by G-d at Mount Sinai	The Torah was composed by the greatest spiritual leaders of their generation.
The Oral Law was also given at Sinai and the Talmud is the form it had developed into by the sixth century.	The Talmud is the new Judaism that the Rabbis invented after the Temple was destroyed
All the Torah mitzvoth and Rabbinic laws must be observed.	Each Jew is free to decide the level of observance that is right for them.
All the 39 prohibitions of Shabbat must be observed.	The spirit of Shabbat demands that work not be done but, for example driving to the synagogue is not an issue.
All the dietary laws in the Torah still apply today.	Kashrut is about hygiene and food that was unhygienic when the Torah was written (pigs, sea foods) are now healthy.
Categories of Jews such as Kohen, Levi, Mamzer are still relevant and will be important when the Temple is rebuilt.	These categories were only relevant in temple times and have no meaning any more.
In synagogues, men and women are divided by a mechitzah (partition)	In synagogues, men and women sit together and women participate in the service and can even be Rabbis.
Hebrew is the only valid language of communal prayer.	Many prayers are said in English.
Two days of Yom Tov are observed outside Israel.	Only one day of Yom Tov is observed everywhere, even on Rosh HaShanah

MAJOR DIVISIONS & INTERPRETATIONS

Religious Studies GCSE: Judaism 1

QUESTION

(a) What does Hasidic mean?

(b) Who was the founder of modern Hasidism?

(c) Name three other Jewish groups.

(d) Explain how the lifestyle of Hasidic Jews and Liberal Jews may be similar and different.

(e) "Differences don't matter. Judaism remains the same." Discuss this statement.

MAJOR DIVISIONS & INTERPRETATIONS

Religious Studies GCSE: Judaism 1

QUESTION

(a) Where did the Reform movement begin?

(b) Who was the founder of Liberal Judaism?

(c) Name three differences between Orthodox and Progressive Jews

(d) Explain the difficulties Jews might have in practicing Judaism in a non-Jewish country.

(e) "It is difficult to be a Jew in a non-Jewish country." Discuss this statement.

MAJOR DIVISIONS & INTERPRETATIONS

Religious Studies GCSE: Judaism 1

TWENTIETH CENTURY HOLOCAUST/SHOAH

The Nazi Holocaust was one of the greatest tragedies of human history. The systematic cold-blooded extermination of six million Jews still traumatises those who lived through those times, their descendants and others. What is particularly shocking about the Nazi holocaust is that:

> so many people died;
> it could take place in a modern democracy;
> so few countries took a stand against it.

MAJOR DIVISIONS & INTERPRETATIONS

Religious Studies GCSE: Judaism 1

HOW DID THE NAZIS COME TO POWER?

These events are well explained in our history books:

Germany were shocked and depressed by their defeat in the 1914-18 World War;

they were humiliated by the reparation payments forced upon them by the Treaty of Versailles in 1919;

runaway inflation, fear of communism and weak governments in the 1920's created a climate in which extremists thrived.

The National Socialist Party (Nazis) grew from a group of dropouts to be a highly effective political party. They used clever propaganda to spread their message and blame, among others, the Jews for the defeat in the war. Even though their original attempt to seize power failed, they continued to expand.

Most Germans were Christians and the medieval mythologies that Jews killed their god and that Jews were guilty of blood libels and well-poisoning was still part of their culture. Nazi propaganda merely extended this religious mistrust of Jews and gave it a political dimension.

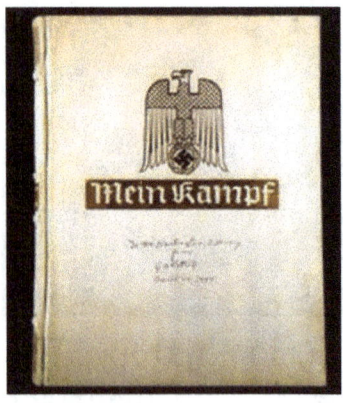

Nazi leader Adolph Hitler wrote a book called Mein Kampf in which he claimed that Aryans (Germans and other Northern Europeans) possessed superior genes to all other races and that it was their duty to create a master race to run the world. This required them to eliminate all those of inferior race. Gypsies, homosexuals, handicapped people and communists all had to be eliminated. But the people at the very bottom of the racial table were the Jews.

Nazi propaganda succeeded in persuading Germans that a vote for Hitler was a vote for German pride and a return to its rightful place as a leading nation in the world. In 1933, the Nazis came to power.

MAJOR DIVISIONS & INTERPRETATIONS

Religious Studies GCSE: Judaism 1

1933-1939 – THE EARLY NAZI YEARS

1 April 1933: a one-day boycott of all Jewish shops and businesses.

1933-35: Jews were regularly dismissed from their jobs and forced to leave the country

1935: the Nuremberg Laws removed German citizenship from Jews and forbade Jews from entering relationships with Aryans

9 November 1938: there was a failed attempt to assassinate the third secretary of the German embassy in Paris. This led to **Kristallnacht** – the Night of Broken Glass. During this pogrom, synagogues were vandalized and Jewish businesses were looted. 91 Jews were killed and thousands more were arrested and taken to Concentration Camps.

July 1938: The **Evian Conference on Refugees.** 32 countries confirmed that few of them were prepared to offer refuge to fleeing Jews. The British Government even prevented Jews from entering Palestine and turned away shiploads of refugees directing them back to Germany.

1938-1939: Austria and Poland annexed to Nazi Germany. New laws forced Jews to wear a **yellow star** on their clothes. This was intended to humiliate and drive Jews further away from Aryan society. It also made it easier to identify them. Jews were then rounded up and **herded into ghettos** where the conditions were appalling.

MAJOR DIVISIONS & INTERPRETATIONS

1939-1945 – THE SECOND WORLD WAR

In the first two years of the war the gradual movement of all Jews under Nazi rule into ghettos and then on to concentration camps was intensified. The Nazi invasion of Soviet Russia finally brought virtually every Jew in mainland Europe under the control of the Nazis. At **Babi Yar** in Ukraine **33,771 Jews were killed** in a single operation on **29-30 September 1941.**

The **Wansee Conference (January 1942)** decreed the **Final Solution** of the Jewish problem, the extermination/elimination of every single Jew: man, woman and child. Millions of Jews were transported in cattle trucks to concentration camps such as **Auschwitz, Dachau and Treblinka.** There they were humiliated, beaten, starved, gassed to death and cremated or buried in mass graves. Had the war not ended when it did who knows how many more than the six million would actually have perished?

Religious Studies GCSE: Judaism 1

THE INFLUENCE OF THE HOLOCAUST

In the immediate years after the Second World War, the Holocaust was the single most influential event in Jewish life. Possibly for the first time since the destruction of the Temple, there was not one single Jew anywhere who was not either directly or indirectly affected by the Holocaust. Every Jew either lost somebody in the Holocaust was a relative of somebody who lost somebody or was a friend of somebody who lost somebody.

The Holocaust led to a number of important changes in the structure of Jewish communal life:

Yeshivot: Virtually all the main Yeshivot had been destroyed in the Second World War. The centre of religious study now moved from Poland/Russia to  the USA and Israel as many Yeshivot were re-established in one or both of these countries. In 1946, Rabbis called for all Jewish boys to go to Yeshivah after finishing school. There was a concerted effort to replace what had been destroyed. In England, a Yeshivah was established in Gateshead which is now one of the foremost Yeshivot in the world.

Outreach: Another call, from the leaders of the Chabad/Lubavitch movement, was to take the Torah to any place where Jews were living. Young couples, known as Shlichim (messengers) were sent to make their home in small towns all over the world to bring comfort and consolation to as many Jewish communities as possible. Today,  there are Chabad centres in over a thousand different cities in the world.

 Absorption: One of the most significant rescue efforts dutring and after the Nazi period was the kindertransport programme that rescued thousands of children from Nazi Europe. England played a major role in this programme as Dr. Solomon Schonfeld organized not just a relief programme but also a system of education and rehabilitation for all these children throughout England.

MAJOR DIVISIONS & INTERPRETATIONS

Religious Studies GCSE: Judaism 1

The State of Israel: For many Jews, the trauma of the Holocaust created an emotional wave of support for the establishment of a Jewish state as a safeguard against another Holocaust. It would be a haven from persecution for any Jew, anywhere in the world. Many non-Jews had similar emotions in the years immediately after the war and, in 1947, the United Nations voted overwhelmingly in favour for the establishment of the Jewish state that is now called Israel.

Changes in Focus: Some Jews feel that since very few other people cared for us during the Holocaust the lesson of the Holocaust is the tremendous importance of **universalism** – if hardly anyone looked out for us during the Holocaust, we must never make that mistake again. We must care about every other persecuted people. Others focus on the need for **Jews to take care of their own** people, since no one else will do it for us.

Religious doubts: For some Jews, the Holocaust made it impossible for them to continue to believe in G-d, for they cannot comprehend how He could abandon them to the Nazi monsters. This led to a growth of Jewish cultural groups that were not religiously observant.

MAJOR DIVISIONS & INTERPRETATIONS

REMEMBERING THE HOLOCAUST

Many Jews feel that it important to remember the events of the Holocaust in order to **honour the memory of those who died.** They also feel that making a special commemoration will help to **prevent anything like it ever happening again.** Different forms of remembrance have been established in the Jewish world:

Holocaust museums: Some have focused their energies on building museums such as **Yad Vashem**, the Washington Holocaust Museum and the exhibition at the Imperial War Museum.

Concentration Camp tours: Many Jews make pilgrimages to Auschwitz and other camps to remember the events that took place there. Just by being in the place where so many Jews died can be a very moving experience.

Holocaust Memorial Days: Memorial days have also been established in memory of the victims. In Israel the 27 Nisan is observed as **Yom HaShoah** – a national Holocaust memorial day. Many Jews around the world join in this memorial commemoration.

Tisha B'Av: Other Jews, however, feel it is more appropriate to remember Holocaust victims on Tisha B'Av, the day that Judaism has already set aside for remembering those who were vicitms of persecution.

British Holocaust Remembrance Day: In Britain, 27 January has recently been established as National Holocaust day for the purpose of remembering the victims and learning the lessons of the Holocaust.

MAJOR DIVISIONS & INTERPRETATIONS

Religious Studies GCSE: Judaism 1

The effects of the Holocaust can still be felt in many families. But as time moves on, many people feel that it is time to look to the future and not to the past. Certainly, the Holocaust should be remembered and its victims should be honoured. Jewish consciousness, however, has always been about building for the future. When the Temple was destroyed the Rabbis legislated for new circumstances and moved on. When great communities were wiped out in the past (at the times of the Crusades and the Spanish Inquisition, for example) new ones were built in their place. Many Jews feel that the lesson of Jewish history is that, whatever has happened in the past, it is the future that counts now. Possibly, the most important lesson of the Holocaust is to educate our children to build a better Jewish world in the next generation.

MAJOR DIVISIONS & INTERPRETATIONS

Religious Studies GCSE: Judaism 1

QUESTION

(a) What does the word 'Shoah' mean?

(b) Describe two ways in which Jews suffered during the Shoah.

(c) Explain three ways in which the Shoah might be remembered.

(d) How does the Shoah affect the lives of Jews today?

(e) "It is time to forget the Shoah and focus our attention on the future." Discuss this statement.

MAJOR DIVISIONS & INTERPRETATIONS

THE LAND AND STATE OF ISRAEL

THE LAND OF ISRAEL

The land of Israel has always been extremely important in Judaism. It was the land to which G-d commanded Abraham to go in Genesis and, when G-d made a covenant with Abraham, He promised this land as an eternal inheritance for his descendants. This promise was repeated to Isaac and Jacob and, following the Israelites slavery in Egypt and 40 years wandering in the desert, it was the land to which Joshua led them after they had received the Torah.

The land of Israel contains all of Judaism's holiest places:

Jerusalem was Israel's capital from the days of King David and was the site of both the First and the Second Temples. The Talmud teaches, based on numerous references in Prophets, that when the Messiah comes the Temple will be rebuilt on the same site.

Religious Studies GCSE: Judaism 1

The Western Wall is the only remaining part of the Temple. This is Judaism's holiest site and it is considered especially meritorious to pray there. Most Jews who visit Israel will make a point of praying at the Western Wall.

The Cave of Machpelah in **Hebron** contains the tombs of Abraham, Isaac and Jacob and of Sarah, Rebecca and Leah. The Talmud states that Adam and Eve are also buried there. There has been a synagogue on the site of this tomb since Biblical times.

Rachel's Tomb lies on the road between Jerusalem and Bethlehem. It is considered an auspicious place to pray when troubles occur.

The tomb of Joseph (which also contained the remains of his sons Ephraim and Menasheh) was in Shechem (Nablus) but sadly it was vandalized by Arabs during the 2000 Intifada and what was salvageable has been removed to Rachel's Tomb. Rachel, of course, was Joseph's mother.

MAJOR DIVISIONS & INTERPRETATIONS

Religious Studies GCSE: Judaism 1

MANY PLACES IN ISRAEL HAVE IMPORTANT HISTORICAL SIGNIFICANCE:

Tiberias in the north of Israel is the place where much of the Jerusalem Talmud was written. It also contains the **tomb of Maimonides**, the greatest halachic authority of the Middle Ages.

Nearby **Safed** was a great Kabbalistic centre in the Middle Ages and was the home of **Rabbi Yosef Caro**, the author of the Shulchan Aruch, for a great part of his life.

A Yeshivah on the Mediterranean coast called **Kerem B'Yavneh** is believed to be on the site to where Israel's supreme court, the Sanhedrin, was relocated after the destruction of the Second Temple.

Further down the Mediterranean coast lies the city of Jaffa, from where Jonah set sail when attempting to avoid going to Nineveh.

MAJOR DIVISIONS & INTERPRETATIONS

Religious Studies GCSE: Judaism 1

MANY OF THE TORAH'S COMMANDMENTS CAN ONLY BE FULFILLED IN THE LAND OF ISRAEL.

Specifically, most of the agricultural laws only apply in the land of Israel. The laws of Shemittah require that every seven years the land lie fallow and no work be done on it. Whatever grows by itself during the Shemittah year has a special holiness. The Torah commands farmers in Israel to separate Terumah (a small tithe) and give it to the Kohanim and Maaser (one-tenth of their crop) and give it to the Levites. All these laws only apply to crops grown in Israel.

One of the 613 commandments in the Torah is to live in Israel. This does not mean that every Jew has an obligation to live there. Rather, it means that those who do are fulfilling a mitzvah. Those who are not able to live in Israel can participate in this mitzvah by supporting and helping those who do live there. Almost all Jews will make a point of visiting Israel at least once in their lives.

MAJOR DIVISIONS & INTERPRETATIONS

THE STATE OF ISRAEL

Many Jews are strongly committed to building and strengthening the State of Israel. **Many non-religious Jews consider the state to be the national home of all Jews,** and so every Jew should support it. **Many religious Jews believe the return of a Jewish state to be a step in the redemption** that will culminate in the arrival of the Messiah. Some even believe that if every Jew went to live in Israel, the Messiah would come immediately.

For many Jews, however, Israel is simply a place where a Jew can be a Jew! The country follows the Jewish calendar in that all Jewish festivals are Bank Holidays. Saturday is the day when the shops are closed not Sunday. Pig-breeding is not allowed in most areas, kosher food is freely available and every town has its synagogues and other places of Jewish interest. **In Israel, there is nothing unusual or different about being a Jew.**

WHY ARE SOME RELIGIOUS JEWS OPPOSED TO THE STATE OF ISRAEL?

There is an opinion in the Talmud that it is forbidden to establish a Jewish State before Messiah comes. Those who follow that view will object to any kind of Jewish State. Others do not object to the principle of a Jewish State but are disappointed with the religious standard of the present Jewish State. They feel a Jewish State must be run according to the laws of the Torah and only those who follow those laws are fit to be its leaders.

HOW MIGHT JEWS SHOW THEIR SUPPORT FOR ISRAEL?

There are many things a Jew can do to show his support for Israel, even if they are not able to live there:

- Buy produce made in Israel
- Support Israeli charities that help poor families
- Donate clothes to Israel for poor families
- Have a tree planted in your name
- Go on holiday to Israel so the money you send boosts Israel's economy
- Spend your gap year there either studying in an Israeli programme or working in a kibbutz or development town.
- Become knowledgeable and involved in Israeli politics
- Celebrate Israeli festivals like Yom Haatzmaut
- Join a Zionist group that increases awareness of Israel's importance

Religious Studies GCSE: Judaism 1

QUESTION

(a) What does the word 'Zionism' mean?

(b) Describe two ways that Jews may show support for the State of Israel.

(c) Give three reasons why a Jew may want to visit the land of Israel.

(d) Explain why many Jews are Zionists

(e) "If G-d is everywhere, Jews do not need a special country." Discuss this statement.

MAJOR DIVISIONS & INTERPRETATIONS

www.ingramcontent.com/pod-product-compliance
Lightning Source LLC
Chambersburg PA
CBHW081618160426
43191CB00012B/2169